"Here is a collection of testimonies written by peop… …ad the courage to put the bottom-line truth to work in their n. …ch story is unique, but the common thread throughout is healing. Brad Blanton's understanding that growth always—and only—moves from the inside out is revealed in the organization of this powerful and inspiring book. Honesty with self, honesty with family of origin, honesty with chosen family, honesty in the workplace, honesty with friends, even honesty with acquaintances—one big, giant, wonderful, courageous ripple effect that will change our lives if we're willing, and just might change the world if enough of us are willing."

—Thom Rutledge
Author of *Embracing Fear & Finding the Courage to Live Your Life*

"The visceral descriptions of anxiety and other painful feelings that come in the process of telling the truth are a key strength of this wonderful book. If you're doing Radical Honesty right, it is messy. And it does often hurt. But, as the stories here show beautifully, if you're willing to go through the mess and the hurt, the rewards are unbelievably, unpredictably rich. The kind of love that is possible after somebody tells the truth (in the way Brad and his colleagues define telling the truth), is a whole different animal—fresher, looser, deeper, sweeter, wilder, stronger—than what usually passes for love."

—Grace Llewellyn
Author of *The Teenage Liberation Handbook,* Co-author of *Guerrilla Learning*

"Just what we need—a book that finally celebrates the healing power of truth! Our culture and world will grow radically different as parents get real with their kids, kids get real with teachers, teachers get real with politicians, and politicians get real with the flowing truth of the world. Thanks, Brad, for your deep commitment."

—Kathlyn Hendricks, Ph.D.
Co-author of *Conscious Loving* and *The Conscious Heart*

"I know that I create it all—you, myself, and all the stuff that goes with it. For me, the trick is in the choices, and creation comes with every little notion. Radical Honesty is nothing more than a means of helping me to lift the veil of my opinion and judgment...a tool to help me wake up from this dream. So that, at last, I can forgive myself, and consequently all others, and love completely. I am the source of all of that."

—Leo Burmester
Actor, *Les Miserables, The Abyss, The Last Temptation of Christ*

"Brad's honesty is so refreshing and liberating. Telling the truth is a radical act. It allows the false to fall away and creates space for the new to arise. Every time I tell the truth, I discover I'm not alone. Such a relief! Brad's books have clarity and grit. He sees the Big Picture (beyond the personal), and at the same time, he plunges into the play of human life with tremendous passion. His work is about true love and living the truth. I recommend his books to all lovers of authenticity."

—Joan Tollifson
Author of *Awake in the Heartland* and *Bare-Bones Meditation*

THE TRUTHTELLERS

Stories of Success
by Radically Honest People

edited by

BRAD BLANTON, PH.D.

www.radicalhonesty.com

Author of

- *Radical Honesty:*
How to Transform Your Life by Telling the Truth

- *Practicing Radical Honesty:*
*How to Complete the Past, Live in the Present and Build a Future with
a Little Help from Your Friends*

- *Radical Parenting:*
Seven Steps To a Functional Family in a Dysfunctional World

Co-Author: Neale Donald Walsch
- *Honest to God:*
A Change of Heart that Can Change the World

Published by
Sparrowhawk Publications
646 Shuler Lane
Stanley, VA 22851
800 EL TRUTH

Cataloging-in-Publication Data:

The truthtellers : stories of success by radically honest people /
edited by Brad Blanton. -- 1st ed.
p. cm.
Includes bibliographical references.
ISBN: 0-9706938-3-4
1. Self-actualization (Psychology). 2. Truthfulness and falsehood.
3. Healing. 4. Psychotherapy.   I. Blanton, Brad. edt   II. Title: Truth
tellers

BF637.S4 B553 2004
158 -- dc21

Cover by Victoria Valentine
Interior Design by Author's Publishing Cooperative and Victoria Valentine
Typeset in Bee-Three, Futura and Book Antiqua
Printed in USA
First Edition

10 9 8 7 6 5 4 3 2 1

CONTENTS

A Ritual to Read to Each Other...

If you don't know the kind of person I am
and I don't know the kind of person you are
a pattern that others made may prevail in the world
and following the wrong god home we miss our star.

For there is many a small betrayal in the mind,
a shrug that lets the fragile sequence break
sending with shouts the horrible errors of childhood
storming out to play through the broken dyke.

And as elephants parade holding each elephant's tail,
but if one wanders the circus won't find the park
I call it cruel and maybe the root of all cruelty
to know what occurs but not recognize the fact.

And so I appeal to a voice, to something shadowy
a remote important region in all who talk:
though we could fool each other, we should consider
lest the parade of our mutual life gets lost in the dark.

For it is important that awake people be awake,
or a breaking line may discourage them back to sleep;
the signals we give— yes or no, or maybe —
should be clear; the darkness around us is deep.

—William Stafford

"I know that I create it all — you, myself, and all the stuff that goes with it. For me, the trick is in the choices, and creation comes with every little notion. Radical Honesty is nothing more than a means of helping me to lift the veil of my opinion and judgement…a tool to help me wake up from this dream. So that, at last, I can forgive myself, and consequently all others, and love completely. I am the source of all of that."

In the fire,
Leo Burmester

That's Why They Call It Personal Growth

"Freedom's just another word for nothing left to lose."
—Kris Kristofferson

We cannot claim to love each other while we withhold information from each other. When we keep our distance from each other by not describing honestly what we have done, what we think, or what we feel, we are maintaining our mutual isolation and alienation from each other. This is the very source of personal and global misery.

Intimacy is not possible without telling the truth. This is one of life's hard lessons; and it is an important one. Lying is a learned form of self–governance and attempted control of others. We have all been taught to lie systematically by schools and parents so we will control ourselves, manipulate each other and submit to control. Overthrowing the internalization of this lifetime of obedience training is overthrowing the government of the mind. We have to overcome our conditioning to be on guard against each other by lying. We have to stop lying in order to learn how to love each other. Unlearning lying as a form of survival turns out to be one of life's greatest inspirations.

I love the job of editing this book. I am so proud of these people and so honored to know them and to be their friend and to have been helped by them and to have helped some of them along the way. We are, and have been, an inspiration to each other. We are a part of our own "Joy Luck Club," to take a beautiful line from Amy Tam and her forbears. Or as Erika Jong so eloquently put it:

> Orgasms of gloom convulse the world;
> & the joy-seekers huddle together.
> We meet on the pages of books & by beachwood fires.
> We meet scrawled blackly in many folded letters.
> We know each other by free and generous hands.
> We swing like spiders on each other's souls.

The hard times we go through do help. They help us to learn about our own courage. They help us to recognize and acknowledge the courage of others. They teach us respect for each other and ourselves. They allow us to be compassionate. The times we have faced the truth, told the truth, and discovered the truth in the process of sharing, give us new and more conscious records for our minds. Records of having told the truth and heard the truth and felt our way through following the truth give us memories of our recent past glory in learning how to forgive and regain the ability to love. Those records remind us that it is possible to continue rediscovering love on a daily basis if we will continue to risk telling the truth.

In my thirty years of experience as a psychotherapist, workshop leader and consultant, it seems to me that what most dramatically transforms a life from normal misery to unreasonable happiness is telling the truth. My first book *Radical Honesty* became a best-seller because a lot of people who started living out loud found out how well it works and started talking about it. All of us together have a message for each other and for any who now join us. Imagine our voices in unison: "We hope you will take this personally. We offer these stories to support you in improving the quality of your life by being inspired to follow our example, and then 'pay it forward.'"

What I talked about in *Radical Honesty* and in my second book, *Practicing Radical Honesty*, and what the storytellers in this book mean by telling the truth, is not what most people call telling the truth. We have realized that most of us, most of the time, are performing. Radical Honesty means admitting that we are usually performing, and doing so in particular specific instances where we cop to our performance and give it up, and tell what is actually going on with us instead.

Many times, every day, we all make up stories about what we did and why we did these things. These stories are automatic. They are ex-post facto rationalizations, done to make us look good in the eyes of other people. Much of the time, quietly inside our own minds, we are looking for a rationalization for lying. Don't pretend that you don't spend a lot of energy on this yourself. If giving up that pretense is hard for you to do, don't feel alone. Read on.

We are telling you stories about interrupting our mind's agenda-to-perform-and-try-to-look-good-through-lying because we want you to know you can't overdo the detail. What happens in these stories of successful transformation is that there is a blow-by-blow description of what happened, what the person speaking thought about what happened, and how he/she felt at the time it happened and how he/she feels about it now. We want you to know that it's important that you tell what you really feel, what you really think and what you really have said and done to the very people you are most inclined to hide this information from. The people you are most afraid of, or intimidated by, or afraid of hurting, or scared of offending, are the very ones we are asking you to take on, and tell the truth to.

Basically that's it. All you have to tell the truth about is what you have done, what you think and what you feel. It's simple. But it is hard to do. It's hard to do because it is so contrary to our conditioning. We have been trained to perform in front of each other and to guard against sharing openly, lest we offend or hurt or embarrass or intimidate or shock or upset or ruffle the feathers of our fellow human beans.

And as you know from accidental revelations in your own life, and as you will see in these stores, people do get their feelings hurt, or get offended or shocked or sometimes unbearably relieved. These things, direly predicted by all the scared teachers of your life, do occur. They were right. But what they didn't discover or failed to tell you was, that when all these feelings occur, if neither you nor the one you are bothering with the truth run away, something wonderful happens. If both of you stay with your experience, and keep on being honest as new reactions occur, right on the other side of the rough going is great freedom and love for each other and a powerful friendship and caring, as beings who love each other, rather than as performers.

Telling the truth is hard, but covering up is harder on you and harder to live with than the truth. Being isolated within our own internally judging minds is what most of us suffer and die from. The rescue from our own minds is done through authentic contact and honest sharing with other human beings. The only way to do this is to do it. Freedom is a psychological accomplishment. People who accomplish freedom, freedom from the jail of their own former minds, are models of what personal growth is all about.

Once caught, the honesty and freedom concept works like a virus. People pass it forward. Love expands its territory. Families are renewed. Communities form. Marriages happen. New beginnings occur.

For about 15 years now, I have been conducting the eight-day Course in Honesty Workshop, to teach people how to be voluntarily vulnerable to this honesty virus. One of the things we do in that workshop is tell the entire story of our lives to each other. These life stories are videotaped and the participants are given the video to take home and show their families and friends. Some of the stories in this book tell what happened when family members or spouses viewed those life stories and then talked about them together. Sometimes at the beginning of that conversation about the past all hell breaks loose. But after that, some wonderfully strange and exciting things happen.

Cases of Mistaken Identity

Our stories have a theme to them. The common thread is successful deliverance from the jail of the mind and the revision of an incorrect belief about who we are. When we discover that we are not our reputations in the eyes of our parents or teachers or peers or bosses or spouses, we also discover the same thing about others. A person with mistaken identity identifies the rest of the people in his life mistakenly. We find out who we are behind the mask of false identity, and simultaneously begin to glimpse the same in those close to us. Once this gets straightened out, authentic conversation can begin. People start getting to know each other candidly when they talk, rather than being paranoid about each other and lying all the time. That's when the feces hits the wind machine. That's when the downfall of the established social order begins. The downfall of the established order, though always feared, is something greatly to be desired. When these "nervous breakthroughs" occur in a couple, in a source family, in a progenitor family, in a business, or in the way the world is governed—a clearing occurs, and a new beginning happens.

Many movies exemplify what the people in this book are talking about. *Secrets and Lies, Courage Under Fire, American Beauty* and *Pay it Forward*, to name just a few, serve to illustrate the transformation that follows from telling the truth. In those movies, when the characters finally have the courage to tell the truth, the resultant difficulties they face are less damaging to everyone than the lies they had been hiding behind. That same kind of transformation has been experienced by literally thousands of real-life graduates of the jail of permanent adolescence our culture calls adulthood. Some of these stories are from people who did my workshops. Some are from people who read one of my books and wrote to me. Some are from people who were in psychotherapy with me and wrote or called or emailed and told me their stories after they began life again by telling the truth.

In almost every case when this extraordinary level of honesty occurs in real life there is a sharing of emotion, a rebirth of intimacy, and a renewal of relationship and psychological healing. And often this happens not only for the truthteller, but also for those hearing the truth. The virus spreads. The world is changing because of this.

As people tell their stories, we who hear them discover the value of undoing our own lies and coming forward with the truth. We all have a message for each other. "Listen to this. This is how I learned to come on out and play and quit hiding. Try it."

We are in alignment with a lot of other great teachers and learners who are doing this work: The Forum, the New Warrior/Woman Within workshops, The Advanced Course, and the Self Expression and Leadership Course of Landmark Education, The Miracle of Love, all the courses run by Gay and Kathlyn Hendricks, The Work by Byron Katie and many other teachers and trainings I will later wish I had mentioned here—they all teach the same thing we are talking about. We all are advocates of, and want to keep inspiring you to grow into, an ongoing new way of being—living out loud from your presence to each moment of life, your presence to your own feelings and your presence to other beings. From this, miracles occur.

Universal Theme of Liberation

These stories of liberation from the jail of the mind have a theme to them that goes back to humanity's earliest recorded history. In his book *The Hero with a Thousand Faces*, the great mythologist and Jungian scholar, Joseph Campbell, spoke about a universal theme present in the mythology of all world cultures, and he called it "the hero's journey;' there are several definitive stages in the journey:

(1) A very unlikely hero (a slave or a hobbit, etc.) has to venture forth into the unknown bearing the burden of saving his kind from destruction.

(2) A great danger must be confronted in order to venture into the unknown. Very fearsome creatures guard the gateway to the unknown. Dragons or gargoyles or demons or other really scary guardians must be faced in all these stories, or there is no story, no breakthrough into the unknown, and no hero. Each hero got the call to venture forth, and they answered the call, no matter how terrifying the guardians at the gate.

(3) The hero must attain something in the land of the unknown and bring it back to the world of the known (the knowledge of the ring thrown into the fire, the golden fleece, the holy of holies, the tablets with the ten commandments, etc.) When this occurs it changes everything. There is great sadness letting go of the past and the realization that things will never again be the same. But there is also great joy, because that new thing which is brought forth is the salvation of the hero's people. Thus, in both personal and universal mythology the "courage" part of encouragement was begun in human history, and the "venture" part of the adventure life was, and can be, exemplified.

The people who tell their stories in this book are heroes. They did just what Joseph Campbell talked about. They were scared to death, but they did it anyway. They told the truth, when they couldn't know what might happen, but feared the worst. They could have been disowned by their family or spouse, been damned and rejected by their loved ones, abandoned by their children, lost their jobs, businesses, money and all their possessions, lost a friend forever, or endured a whole panoply of lesser evils. But they did what they needed to do. They came clean. They wanted intimacy. They didn't want "getting along as usual." They didn't want the eternal dance on eggshells to maintain "peace" until they could finally die having "managed" their lives so that no one was ever upset by the truth. They didn't want to sit on their feelings, lie about what they had done, hide what they thought, or manipulate those around them by playing to the audience, and avoiding, at all costs, having to face the demons at the gates. They received the call, to speak what was so, and they came forth. They are shining examples. They offer both encouragement and confrontation for all the people who got the call and ran away, and are still suffering their cowardice in the hell of their own secret minds. We offer these stories to those who are being called upon right now, and to those who have avoided the call, and know it.

We also offer these stories to former heroes who chickened out again later, when they somehow forgot who they were, and fell back on their reputations to themselves as an excuse for inaction in a new moment. It is never too late. It's never too late to be a hero. It is never to late to rediscover love. Until the moment you are dead, you have the possibility of being truly alive.

This is the main point we all want to make: No matter how often your mind takes over again and recaptures the space of freedom from your noticing being, you can break out of that jail when you dare to tell the truth again. Truthfulness sets you free. Radical honesty in your family liberates you from the jail of your own mind in your family. Radical honesty at work liberates you from the jail of your own mind at work. Radical honesty in your intimate relationships liberates you from the jail of your own mind in those relationships. Radical honesty in the world changes how the world is organized.

These stories tell us that liberation from our own minds is the ultimate freedom we human beings can have. The noticing being that each of us is, who lives in jail a lot of the time, gets release time now and then for good behavior. Good behavior is simply noticing and reporting, without editing, what we feel, what we think and what we have done. We call this Radical Honesty because it is unusual and distinct from what people usually think of as telling the truth. It is hard to do because it goes against the grain of how we were all raised. We have all been taught systematically to lie by our culture. Our parents and teachers and role models consistently taught us to lie, and even though we were told not to lie, we learned, by how we were treated, to do just that.

The Constant Rediscovery of Our True Identity

I like to use Catholic parochial school as a model here, having spent so much time as a psychotherapist with recovering Catholics. When those nuns, like many other teachers and parents, scared, and threatened and manipulated children to play like they were "good little boys and good little girls" at all times, and at any cost, they were teaching them how to lie. The big lie, which sources and justifies all the little white lies which make up the jail of alienation most of us live in, is that *who we are is our performance.* As we grow from childhood to adulthood the messages are constantly there to tell us how and who to be. Starting way before kindergarten, we are taught that who we are is defined by how we behave, what we do, how we perform. From that point forward we are the grades we make, what our teachers think of us, what our peers think of us, what group we name ourselves a part of, what team we are on, our reputation in the community, how much money we make, what kind of car we drive, what company we work for, what work we do, etc. Closely aligned with that, and also important to maintaining our performance and reputation, is that whatever we can sell as real to other people will in fact be real for us. I pretend therefore I am.

The horrific child abuse that passes for normal middle class education and parenting is a lie. Children must go through this brainwashing for submission to authority and pretend to like it. The abuse, usually called "education," is justified by wholesale belief in one, unfortunately incorrect, assertion articulated by Descartes when he said, "I think, therefore I am." He was wrong. I am, therefore I think is a more functional view. Thinking is secondary to being. Until that correction is made, most human lives will continue to remain miserable. War will continue on ad infinitum as will the struggle between the haves and have-nots, starvation, poverty, disease, greed and the misery within the mind that happens regardless of material circumstances.

What adds insult to injury is that those folks who lied to us, and to whom we have lied, are the people we have to forgive in order to go on with our lives. They are the people we have to complete with, personally, in order to gain our own freedom from the jail of ignorance in which we have all mutually suffered. Freedom is a psychological accomplishment which takes courage and hard work. Our freedom requires that we *forgive* the folks we are mad at, whether they change their behavior or not. We have to get over our attachment to our story rather than try to change them. That is the current frontier of heroism. Fortunately, when such forgiveness occurs, positive change usually does happen, both for the truthteller and for the people who have been told the truth.

Our freedom also requires that we get over the idealization of parents, parental figures and other people who have done right by us. We can do that by appreciating and acknowledging them for the kindness and care they have shown us, and then getting over it! Whether we are mad and specifically resent them for what they did, then follow through until our feelings change to openness, or loving and specifically appreciating them for what they did, the task is essentially the same. We have to get over our attachments to both hate and love stories, by actually experiencing hate and love, by honestly telling folks what we both resent them and appreciate them for, while in their presence, in order not to be victims of our own stories of the past.

The liberation from the jail of our own mind comes when we end up sitting in a room across from a person who was a former enemy, or a former kind caretaker, or both, and have the strange experience of no longer having any axes to grind or glories to exemplify; we then find ourselves open to a new experience with them from the space of simple presence and possibility. This is what forgiveness is. It is getting over your emotional attachments to the meaning the people from your past have for you, and simply being present to them and available for whatever happens next. Out of this comes the power to make things happen in the world in a brand new way.

Forgiveness for the sake of your own freedom to create your future anew is hard work, and it is a model for a level of maturity most of us have been unable to reach so far in our adolescent society. The matter has now become critical. Because our technology and environmental interference has out paced our personal and societal growth to such an extent that our self extermination is likely, the skill of forgiveness is now necessary for our survival.

Sometimes This Doesn't Work

Radical Honesty doesn't work, without fail, a hundred percent of the time. Being radically honest sometimes fails to accomplish what the person attempting to be honest anticipated. Formulated in brief, the slogan for our commercial is: "Radical Honesty! It works pretty good! ...Most of the time!" We are not saying that in all cases honesty always works out and everyone lives happily ever after. We are saying that it works quite well most of the time. As Old Lodgeskins, the chief, in the movie *Little Big Man* said, "Sometimes the magic works, and sometimes it doesn't." So we *do* have a few examples in this book of how things didn't turn out as well as expected or as soon as expected, etc. However, we were hard pressed to find any examples of negative results. Sometimes in the process of telling the truth, at certain stages, the going gets pretty rough (and the language gets a little rough too in a lot of these stories), and now and then people run away from the truth of their experience. Sometimes the going got rough about half way through when big lies were revealed, but generally, as you will see, things eventually worked out fine. Things worked so well, in fact, the enemies fell in love again, or I should say, fell into presence to each other again. And it became contagious. In fact it may happen to you from reading their stories.

You Never Know Until You Know

These stories are from heroes who faced the demons at the gates at the end of adolescence and entered into the unknown, even at the risk of being cast out of relatedness forever. These are stories of forgiveness, of lightening up, of people becoming available to each other and open to each other after a long time of just being categories to each other based on fear, hate and romantic idealism rather than reality. These are stories of the ultimate accomplishment of the great Buddhist goal of compassion. When we get over our attachment to our stories about each other and ourselves we become present to each other with compassion.

This is the best book I have ever written, probably because, most of it, I didn't write. These stories were written by people who lived them — who took risks, learned to forgive and learned how to love. Through all the edits and reorganizations (and there were many, and many people who helped me with them) it was not possible for any of us to keep from being moved to tears even when we had read the stories several times. The magnanimity of the human spirit shows through here, to make up a portion of the real "people's history" of our times. It is a history of the transcendence of ignorance and suffering and the victory of love, over and over again. Granted, because of our honesty, we are not normal people. We are average people who are just truthtellers. But we are the last hope for humankind.

Enjoy falling in love with these courageous people. Rejoice if you get the virus. Pass it forward.

— Brad Blanton
Sparrowhawk Farm
September 2003

PART ONE

SETTLING THINGS AT THE SOURCE
Radical Honesty in the
Family of Origin
—Mothers, Fathers, Brothers Sisters

"At the core of every moral code there is a picture of human nature, a map of the universe, and a version of history. To human nature (of the sort conceived), in a universe (of the kind imagined), after a history (so understood), the rules of the code apply."
— Walter Lippman

"Telling the truth allows a person to change the code with which their life is programmed."
— Brad Blanton

2

LIZ:

How I Came To Radical Honesty and Grew Up in Two Hours (Plus 48 Years)

It's New Year's Day, and I'm thinking about the past year and all the changes it brought. There was a move from Omaha to Kansas City and a job change, both of which were major. But without a doubt, the most significant thing that happened in the last year is that I finally grew up by learning about Radical Honesty.

In April (I believe), with nothing better to do, I dropped by Barnes & Noble to hear some guy named Brad Blanton talk about a book that sounded interesting: *Radical Honesty*. The talk was free, so I thought, what the hey. As Brad talked in his inimitable way, I was amazed by his whole presentation: physical, mental, and emotional. I'd never seen, met or even heard of anybody like this before. I imagined he was the most honest, present-in-the-moment person

I'd ever seen, without the self-righteousness, airy-fairiness or solemnity of a lot of New Age fakers. He didn't proclaim that he had The Answer, freely admitted to borrowing ideas from others, yet had an air of confidence that made the humility attractive.

This Radical Honesty thing was something that was never practiced in my home when I was growing up. Everything negative was shoved under the rug, resentments were never spoken of; there was a stale, dead, toxic feel to the household that literally made me sick when I was a child. In Brad Blanton's life, I imagined, things were different, fresh, honest, free. Whatever Brad Blanton had, I wanted some of it. I didn't even stay to meet him, because I knew I would see him again. I signed the mailing list, bought the book, read it, and when I got a notice about the 2-day workshop in Indianapolis in July, I went for it without hesitation.

At the 2-day workshop the hot-seat work was intense, and I got in touch with a load of rage toward my mother. I became vulnerable, not an easy thing for me, and the support of the other people in the group was touching. I noticed that everybody became wonderful when they were vulnerable and told the truth.

As I listened to Brad's teaching sessions, I found myself making connections between many disciplines and "truths" I had learned following the New Age path. There were familiar elements, but now Brad was putting it together in a way that seemed practical and actually useful. Brad was teaching me how the mind works (like a bullshit-making or a meaning-making machine) and how to free myself from the prison of my own mind. That had been the missing piece I'd been searching for for nearly 20 years on a spiritual path.

By the end of the 2-day, I knew I had to do my completion with my mother. I was filled with dread at the thought of it, but I knew I couldn't not do it: I was a pressure cooker filled with boiling, toxic rage, and I was close to blowing up. The anger was poisoning my relationships with everybody in my life, including myself. It was adversely affecting my job. The completion had to be faced — later. After the 8-day in September, maybe.

If I wondered beforehand whether the 8-day Course in Honesty workshop would be worth the money and time, when it ended, I knew that what I had gained there was beyond price. What I had gotten was a chance to be real, tell my story and get over it and get on to the life I wanted. When I got home and looked at my life story on videotape (after being afraid to for two weeks), I was grief-stricken. This is how I am? I don't like her. I don't want to be her. It was clear that I had been living according to my mind's distorted "story" about how things were, a story filtered through rage. I saw my whole life as a tragedy of "what might have been if only." I needed to get over this victim story and literally get real. It was time to do the completion with my mother.

How simple it all seems now, but how difficult it seemed before doing it. On the three-hour drive to my mother's house, I felt alternate waves of despair and excitement. Every time I feared doing the completion work "wrong," I remembered Brad's advice to "do it all wrong, do a third-rate job, and fuck it all up." Most of my life, I've been immobilized by perfectionism, so this idea of intentionally doing something badly (if that's how I had to do it to get it done) was a new wrinkle. Risking looking crazy, looking ugly, being judged, causing my mother a heart attack, etc., etc., were some of the fears I had to fight down. As I drew closer to Jeff City, I felt the way I felt when I was coming down with the Hong Kong flu but didn't realize it yet: I knew something was about to happen, and I wasn't sure exactly what it was, but I suspected it would be something pretty serious and bad.

When I arrived, grim and tense, I explained to my mother what I was going to do, why I needed to do it, and how. I requested that she sit at the kitchen table and listen to me speak my resentments and appreciations to her. I requested that she not interrupt, and I told her that I would listen to what she had to say afterward. She agreed.

For the next two hours, I talked, yelled, screamed, stood up, sat down, paced around, cried, pounded on the table for emphasis, said "fuck," "shit," "damn," "God-damn," and "hell." Numerous times. This to a little old lady Christian Scientist. I told her I had sex with men I wasn't married to, and that I enjoyed it and saw nothing wrong with it. I told her I did drugs. I told her every stupid resentment I could think of — 48 years of resentment spewed out in two hours.

Then it was my mother's turn to talk. During my rant, she had mostly listened, but occasionally her jaw dropped, and she said, "Whaaat??" or "I don't remember that." It became clear that her remembrance of my childhood and hers were radically different. For instance, she was resentful over my not having involved her in preparations for my first wedding. She said I was very snotty to her. I didn't remember that, but allowed that it probably was because I didn't like her. There was silence for a moment, then she said quietly, "I didn't like my mother, either." I was stunned. My mother had never revealed herself like that to me before. I felt something open up inside me. I wouldn't call it love, exactly, but it was a flow of energy toward my mother.

At one point, my mother started crying, and she talked about how she wasn't going to live much longer, and now, in light of what I had said, she thought she should change her will and take my name off her house and her stock accounts. She said when she died, she didn't want a notice in the paper or a funeral, just a cremation, and that she didn't want anybody to know, and she didn't want anybody to tell me, because nobody cared. I told her I resented her for saying those things at that moment, and that I imagined she was trying to manipulate me. She knocked it off, and we went on to talk more calmly.

All in all, I give myself a C+ rating for how I did the completion (Hooray for average!), and I give my mother an A-. She was willing to withstand the toxic rage assault, and before I left, we cried together, hugged and kissed. And this time, I really wanted to hug her. I had revealed myself to her, and to the extent she could, she had revealed herself to me. I felt as if we were no longer in some set mother-daughter act, but had transcended that and were now two human beings, just being with each other. Amazingly, I felt as if I'd grown from a splintered, self-centered, petulant child into a whole, caring adult in two hours.

On the road back home, I felt as if a fresh breeze was blowing through my mind and body. It was a brilliant, sunny day. The sky was a deep autumn blue that was perfectly clear and seemed filled with unlimited potential. I felt energized, excited, light and restless. I really could have used a good reggae band to dance my brains out to. Since finding one along I-70 seemed a remote possibility, I wondered what else I could do to satisfy this tingling, excited, vital urge to do something.

First, I stopped at a C-store, bought a package of Hostess Snowballs and a Diet Dr. Pepper. In the car, I wolfed down one of the Snowballs and slugged down some Diet Dr. Pepper, but as I kept on driving, I thought, "Well, that wasn't it. What else? What else? What do I need?"

Then I found myself making some strange sound I'd never made before. It was somewhere between singing and yelling. It was a pure, focused sound that created overtones, as in Tibetan throat-singing. That was really fun. I enjoyed the sounds for a while, then thought, "That wasn't it, either. What do I need?" Then it came to me: a Swisher Sweet. I wanted to smoke a Swisher Sweet cigar. Where that idea came from, I don't know. I'd never smoked one in my life. My first ex used to smoke them. So I stopped at a C-store and bought some. On the way back out to the car, I fumbled with the cellophane. Adrenaline was rushing, and I broke the first one trying to get it out of the box. The second one came out okay, and I lit it, rolled down the window, drew in a mouthful of warm, pungent smoke, blew it out and sighed, "Aaaaaah!" That was it. I drove down I-70 with the plastic tip of the Swisher Sweet clamped between my teeth, feeling like FDR. As the smoke billowed out the window, I felt a profound feeling of peace, joy and well-being.

In the following week, I did completions with Winston, the guy I'd been involved with in Iowa City, and with my friend, Lynn. After each one, I felt another layer of bullshit and mind-weight had been lifted. I felt cleaner, stronger, more okay about myself.

The healing of my relationship with my mother is still evolving. When I left after our completion, I didn't know how I felt about her. I had no idea what came next, now that the Big Event was over. When I saw her at Thanksgiving, I noticed I was being more solicitous and protective toward her. I felt affectionate toward her. Then at Christmas, I was practically overwhelmed with feelings for her. Lately, I have been feeling a love for her that is so deep it hurts. I believe I am grieving. I have regrets that I didn't clear with her years ago, before she began to deteriorate physically. We might have enjoyed trips together, or just simply being together much more. Even though I have regrets, I also have gratitude that even though it took a long time, eventually I got my mother back. She didn't change; I did.

Before, looking at my childhood through a glass darkly, as it were, painting everything black and bad, I couldn't see the good. Now that the resentment has been released, I can see the good. Now I feel grateful to have had the parents I had. I remember the way I thought of the past, but now I'm not attached to it. I see quite clearly that it was a story, not reality. The facts I remembered were accurate in most cases, but because I was stuck in a negative paradigm, I omitted any facts that contradicted the story that I'd had a lousy, lonely childhood.

The fact is, I had two parents who loved me imperfectly. So did everybody. They did some things very well, others not so well. I've gotten off that "they should have known better" judgment. Now I think they did pretty well, all things considered. I always had clean clothes, enough food, a nice house in a safe neighborhood, a mother who was there when I got home from school, and nobody got hit or screamed at or hauled off to jail. My parents encouraged me to learn, to be curious, to think. They gave me riding lessons, ballet and tap, piano lessons, art classes, etc., etc. They took me to museums and music concerts, and we went on vacations. My mother read to me, my dad used to make up stories about a mouse family and draw pictures of the mice that made me laugh. When my dad went on business trips, he would bring me dresses from Saks Fifth Avenue or Stix Baer & Fuller or other nice stores. And I think all of that is pretty Goddamned wonderful.

The year 1997 has been the most significant in my life, as that was when I finally reached adulthood in just two hours plus 48 years, by practicing Radical Honesty. I reclaimed my love for my mother, thereby reclaiming my ability to love myself and others. That's the most important and glorious Christmas gift I can imagine.

I still have a couple of completions to do, and I'm just as frightened about doing them as I was about doing the first one. In the coming year, I am working on getting better at staying current and living out loud, figuring out how to use Radical Honesty at work, writing up projects and finding committed listeners to help me get them done.

Thank you to Brad, Amy, Carsie and Elijah, and all of you in my workshops. I appreciate you for having taught me, supported me, hugged me, listened to me, resented and appreciated me. I feel in my heart that this next year will be an incredible year of growth—not the horrible, painful kind, but the positive, exciting kind—for all of us.

I love you all.

Liz

Liz Craig lives and works in Kansas City. She is in business for herself as a freelance consultant doing public relations and problem solving for businesses.

3

PATRICIA:
Excerpts From
My Journal

E ditor's Note: These excerpts from Patricia's journal came about four or five months after her participation in a Course in Honesty Eight Day Workshop. Part of this particular workshop had been videotaped for John Stoessel's first story about Radical Honesty on the television show, 20/20. Patricia had done a lot of work on completing things with her family since her participation in the workshop by the time the story aired, and the excerpts that follow here are from her journal entries just before, and then just after, seeing herself on TV, in segments taped several months earlier.

January 9:

I am sitting on the couch in our suite in the inn. I am tired this morning. I have a headache. I have my period. I am lounging by the fire and I am filled with Spirit. I am peaceful.

My heart is full. I am thinking of Mom. Each time I think of her now I feel such a pressure in my chest. I feel tears well up in my eyes. I cry. The depth of this love, this compassion I feel for my Mom actually hurts. I haven't felt this before. It flows through my body. And I am fully getting how much Mom loves me.

I resented my Mom because I think she is unemotional, she is not real affectionate, she always has lists of doings and things to achieve, she often says that something she did is not good enough, she often says that things could be better, she is often worried about what other people think, she is worried about what will happen, she is always worried about money, she is always worried.

I have resented her because I am so much like her. I learned these worries from her. And I learned them through many generations before her. This is the legacy: feeling so alone that all I can do is worry. I imagine Mom feels the same way. I imagine everybody feels the same way. We are all searching for the feelings of divine connection. As I see it, this legacy came from thousands of years of being suppressed, notably the feminine spirit in women but also in men. I can see this in our lost connection with the Earth, our Great Mother. After all these generations and growing up in a world like this, I can see how difficult it is for Mom or anyone else to have done it any differently. And now I see that my Mom and I are definitely making a difference. We are feeling our pain, exposing it and finding love and compassion to create it differently.

When I think back on all that I shared with Mom, particularly my resentments, first I felt heroic for acknowledging myself — then I felt disgusted for being arrogant and thinking that I'm better than her. Now I feel communion, in unity with her as a fellow priestess on our journey home. I feel complete now. I realize how deeply I love and cherish my Mom for her courage to transcend the legacy which I imagine was passed to her by her own mother. I was blinded to my Mom's pain by my own pain, resentment and anger. Now, in sharing my pain and judgments with her honestly, I have awakened to see her...

Through these past months Mom has listened to every word I have said, and has accepted me with open arms every time I have come home. She has withdrawn at times in anger and fear and yet she has not walked away. She returns each time, more open and loving. She has never abandoned me when I have expressed my pain, my blame and my resentments.

At 71 she is spry and beautiful, and still teaching with an aliveness that keeps me thinking that she is 40. Through our recent months of sharing, she has acknowledged her daughters, acknowledged our pain and looked courageously at her own. Her tears have flowed and her resistance and regrets have given way to hugs and kisses. I am overwhelmed by her courage recently to admit that she is an alcoholic.

We are truly sisters in the journey. I embrace her as my kindred spirit and see her no longer as the unloving critical mother, but as a true priestess in all her sacred power forging onward, as I am, to her full expression as feminine spirit, a nurturing, creating, loving goddess. I imagine now that Mom would cringe reading these words and possibly think it is blasphemous to call ourselves goddesses. Yet, I trust that within her is the listener in her soul who knows this to be true.

January 17:

I didn't sleep last night. After watching the 20/20 segment on Radical Honesty, which included scenes from the tape they made of our workshop, I felt sad and kept thinking about my Mom. The show seemed so dramatic. Pieces and statements were put together in such a way, SO out of context that the story became untrue for me. The story about me was that I blamed my Mom for my life's pain and my marriage. I was asked in the interview if I blamed my Mom and I said, "NO. This process is not about blame. It is about me taking responsibility for the choices I have made in my life which have caused me both pain and joy." If I blame her, I become focused on her and relinquish my own power to change the course of my life. Although I have blamed my Mom in the past, that is not how I feel towards her now. It is clear to me that blame has been a symptom of my fear. I was afraid to look at myself, afraid of responsibility and so it was easier to blame her. I have had anger and resentments that I wanted to let go of so I could be more intimate with her and create a more joyful life.

All I could think of was how close I feel to Mom and how this show might upset her and threaten what we had created over these past three months. Having shared my resentments and anger with her, I feel so released and free to show her how much I love her. Our relationship has been transformed (not to mention my relationship with the rest of the family). These past three months have been a lot of work, processing, traveling home, going to workshops, practicing Radical Honesty at work, in my romantic relationships and with my family, having family meetings and even working through a family crisis together.

As a family we have shared a lot and our relationships are more open, honest and intimate. It feels so wonderful. That doesn't mean that our family relationships will always be easy or light. We still have our ways of generating dysfunction; however we are more aware and have created the opportunity to make changes in the way we relate to each other.

Our relationships are more truthful and loving. I absolutely love Mom and my family with all my heart. I get what unconditional love is now. Not that I feel it all the time towards my family, but I have felt it, and that is miraculous. I feel light; as if I've put down a 300-pound sack I've been carrying on my back most of my life. I feel what I imagine my Mom feels towards her children — total love and acceptance. Now, after this show, I was scared it would cause a rift between Mom and me. My mind started to go crazy thinking of all that she might have been feeling and imagining, what she might have been thinking. When talking with David (my significant other) earlier, he reminded me that I was making this all up in my own head. Hadn't Mom and I gotten to a new place? Yes. "Trust that," he said.

I went to bed and couldn't sleep. I was filling up with self-doubt. I wanted to call David back at 2:30 a.m. his time. I kept obsessing about how hurt my Mom must be and that I didn't mean for it to go this way. I kept thinking about how angry my brothers and sisters must be. I felt awful. I kept thinking about how people would be angry with me — that selfish, angry bitch of a daughter! Ugh! I felt caught between two worlds. In one I was to blame for the new pain I imagined everybody was experiencing. In the other I was a confident, brave woman fighting for her soul...

I was not having fun with my mind alone in bed in the middle of the night. I couldn't take it. I wanted to call David. I turned on the bedside lamp and the bulb blew out. I thought, "Fuck this," sign or no sign, I was still going to call. I picked up the phone and started to dial. Then I heard my inner voice: "Wait a minute. You're going to bother him for something you decided to do knowing there would be some uncomfortable consequences?" Suddenly I realized that by calling him I was giving up my own power. I alone had to face the consequences. I meditated and finally fell asleep. I woke at 3:00 a.m. and couldn't sleep. I kept thinking about my Mom. It was 6:00 a.m. her time I watched the minutes go by. At 3:25 a.m. I called home, imagining Mom would be hurt or angry, and trusting that she would still love me anyway.

The phone rang twice. "Hi Mom. Hi Trish." And at the same time we both said, "How are you? Are you OK?" My God, my heart soared. My mother is such a blessed person. I felt humbled by her graciousness, love and warmth.

She kept saying, "We tried to call you last night. How are you doing?"

"Mom, I'm so sorry. I had so hoped it wouldn't come out that I blamed you so much."

"Patricia, please. Not to worry. That's T.V. I knew what was going on. I know you. I know what you have done for this family these past few months. Oh, how can we thank you? Nothing can take that away. It was tremendous."

I said, "God, I couldn't believe how many times they showed me yelling."(Mom laughed) "Yeah, well, your father, sister and I laughed when, after the third time, your sister said she wanted to be your agent. (We laughed) I thought you looked beautiful. One time when you turned your head, your hair looked gorgeous."

"Mom, I appreciate you guys for laughing, for not getting upset and for taking it in such a light way." At that moment I felt so loved by Mom, so free, so full of light. I asked her again how she felt about it. She said, "Fine, OK."

So do I.

Patricia is an author and a fitness expert. Her work with people on their physical health and well being has been greatly enhanced by her courageous instigation of completion and feeling her way through to forgiveness of her mother.

4

CRISTYN:
Memories and
Realities of Abuse

Over seven years ago I started thinking that I had been sexually abused by my dad and possibly that my mom was watching. I had all sorts of wild memories coming into my mind. I got really scared and paranoid. For six months, the only two people who knew where I lived were the 82 year-old gentleman I lived with, and one friend of mine who told me I could stay at his house if I needed a place to stay. No one had my home phone number. I had a block placed on it. I had voice mail and a post office box.

That was the degree of fear I was in. I was afraid of "them," whoever "they" were, and afraid of my parents tracking me down. If there was a car behind me when I was driving home, I'd get really scared and I'd go so far as to pull over until they passed or I'd drive past my house as many miles as it took until I was convinced that they weren't following me any longer. I lived in the mountains next to a creek in an isolated area. I was constantly hyper-vigilant and wary of what was going on around me. That was the safest place I'd ever lived and the safest I'd ever felt.

I started getting involved in Radical Honesty practice groups. When I saw Brad, in workshops and in visits here, he confronted me several times about me avoiding talking to my parents again. His efforts were met with tantrums and crying. I would sob for days thinking, "How can he even say that? I'm not going to do that. If they die, I'm not going to fucking give a damn! This is me and my world and they can go to Hell!"

Finally, about four years after I had stopped talking to my parents, I asked Taber (a Radical Honesty trainer who lived in my town) if he would mediate a conversation between me and my parents. At the first mediation, my mom was there but my dad wouldn't come. Todd (my mate) was there and my two sisters were there also.

I told my mom I resented her for all the times she said she was going to leave my dad and get a divorce. I resented her for all the times that she stayed, and all the times that she cried and complained about how physically abusive and mean my dad was but then acted "lovey-dovey" for a few days after the big explosions. I resented her for being in the room with him behind closed doors, being in the shower with him in the middle of the afternoon and for spending time with him after those big explosions.

I had found out from one of my sisters when I was 25, that my mom had gotten breast implants. I resented the Hell out of her for not telling me. She got them when I was seven or eight years old. I resented her for all the times that she didn't say anything when I said things like, "Oh when I'm older, I'm going to get breasts like Mom."

Five months earlier I had told my sisters all the specifics of what I had remembered and all the details of why I thought I had been sexually abused. There were dreams I'd had for years, and periods when I lived with that older man, where I would just stay alone rocking and crying when feelings came up, and I found myself covering my crotch and breasts, saying, "Don't touch me. Leave me alone."

I had also spoken previously to other people who had been sexually abused and it explained so much to me including my wild dreams, feelings in my body and the moments of craziness I'd had. I could really relate to these people and also to people who were borderline manic personalities. They seemed like buddies. I thought, "Oh my God, we're from the same planet." I had gone into hypnotherapy then, seeking answers. The therapist, who was a nun, asked me if I'd ever been sexually abused. I took her question as a confirmation that I had been sexually abused.

At the time of the first session with my mom, mediated by Taber, we didn't talk about the sexual stuff, just about the other things that I'd been pissed off about for years but had never told her. Her reaction was just to cry and get into a victim space and say that she'd had to live with my dad and put up with all that.

I said, "No fucking way, you stayed. It was your choice."

After I took the 8-day workshop, I went back and sat her down again. My dad said that I had "bashed" my mom and wanted to know if I was going to "come to talk with us and bash us some more with this Radical Honesty stuff?" I told her a lot of things that I was still pissed off about. Every time she started crying I told her I resented her for crying and for saying, "Your father is such an awful guy, he's so controlling. He won't let me have any money. I'm really poor." I said, "I resent you for saying that! You're such a powerful woman to keep this kind relationship the same for 35 years! I mean that takes a fucking powerful person to keep something exactly the same."

I also said, "You are so talented..." She had been an interior designer. She had worked for management companies. She is an incredible watercolor artist. I said, "Give me a fucking break! You can go out and make as much money as you want right now!" She is very charming. She could attract a really wealthy man much nicer than my dad, too. So, every single time she came back with "poor me" I resented her for it and I said, "You're a fucking powerful woman, don't give me any more of this shit."

Then I'd check in and ask her, "Do you resent me for that?" In the first session, three years ago, I think she managed one or two good resentments she had about me. She started laughing and then crying again, then getting a little bit mad. I used the word "fuck" as much as possible because it offends her terribly. She is so offended by the word "fuck." I said, "Well, resent me for it!"

I'm more forward with her now, and tell her how I feel when she gets into that whiney place. Sometimes I resent her but I also have more tolerance for her being in that place now. If she starts getting whiney I don't have as many sensations in my body. More and more, she's just a human being going through her shit and I'm feeling more detached. She's just this person and I am really where I am because I am. There are still more memories coming up and feelings about being alone. I have more to complete with her. More to grieve. Right now I'm still resenting her for the fake boobs, for not telling me, because I expected to look like that. I'd blossomed late and I'd had lots of teasing about being 'flat as a pancake.' But we are in a place now where we can work through these things.

Well, about two weeks later, Taber was leaving town and I got really panicky because my dad still hadn't come to talk. I called Dad up on the phone. I was terrified. We hadn't spoken in four years. I said, "I am terrified of you and I'm tired of walking around the streets terrified that I'm going to run into you and see you. I'm afraid of being afraid. I imagine I'm really pissed off with you about a lot of things and I really want to get together with you and get over this." I said, "I don't know what this is going to look like but I want to start a conversation and a new relationship with you."

He said, "If this will make you happy, I will come and do this for you. I will go through this bashing just like you bashed your mom, but I will do it for you." So, he came out. As it happened I was really sick and I didn't get as mad at him as I had at my mom during his first meeting. I resented him for saying that I was perfect except for my one flaw, that I stuttered. I resented him for all the times he wouldn't listen to me unless I spoke to him without stuttering. It was a therapy somebody told them to try. I resented him for the way he talked to my mom and calling her "a piece of shit" all the time. I resented him for hitting me over the head, which he still doesn't remember. I was 13 years old and I was standing in the doorway of the garage. I said something to him and "Wham!" I saw stars. I resented him for that and for an incident, in which my mom, my sisters and I sat paralyzed with fear on the couch while my dad pounded on my brother's door, then hit him with a belt. I also resented my mom for not doing anything.

I still feel full of emotion when I say that. I feel my eyes watering, and my throat feels shaky. I thought: I still feel responsible for what happened to my brother, sisters, that I should have protected them from my dad's rage—that I should have been able to run away with them and take them someplace safe. I used to feel that way about my mom too but now I think, "She's fucking on her own. She's still there with that asshole." Her excuse was that she couldn't leave because of the kids. We all went to college and she was still there. That was a big fucking disappointment. She was still with him.

I did some completion work with my sisters and I told them about the experiences that brought me to the conclusion that I was sexually abused. Soon after that conversation, I was at my parent's house for a day and my father didn't look at me or talk to me, so I asked, "What's up? Are you mad at me or something?"

He said, "Yeah, any father would be if they were accused." My sisters had stopped talking to him for a couple of weeks and he asked my mom why. My sisters had told my mother that I thought he had molested me or that something sexually inappropriate had happened. I said, "OK, then let's talk about it and I'll tell you all the details about how I came to that conclusion." I said, "I want to get over this."

He just kept washing the car. He wouldn't look at me or answer me, so I asked, "OK, when do you want to meet to talk about this?"

He said, "Well I don't know when."

I said, "By when will you know when?"

He replied, "Well I'm not going to tell you."

So I started saying, "Well, who sexually abused me then? Who fucking did this? Why am I going through all this stuff?"

He was saying, "Be quiet because of the neighbors."

He was really concerned that the neighbors would hear. I said, "OK, well Brad doesn't think that I was sexually abused. Brad thinks that I'm very gullible and suggestible. He's a Ph.D. And I'm not sure either, so let's talk about this so we can get sure of something. Brad says that if I tell you all the details face to face and sit here with you that the truth will start to come through. Who knows what will happen."

With that, he said, "OK, I'll come in."

He came in and we had a three-hour long conversation. I started going back to the story of what happened seven years ago when I was around people who had been sexually abused and others who were DID (disassociated identity disorder) and I said, here's what happened to me. I had these wild dreams, wild sensations in my body, weird shit going on in my sexual relationships—he didn't want to hear about my sexual relationships so that was a stretch.

Todd (my boyfriend, also a participant in Radical Honesty groups) was coaching me because I kept losing track of where I was. I talked about how terrified I was as a kid, how I hid in the closet, what I felt when I was around my dad, and how I felt in my body when he said certain things. I told him the main scene I remembered was standing in the shower with him, looking at his genitals and feeling scared. Lots of feelings and sensations coming up about that. I told him that I had an image of his penis in my mouth and feeling like something bad was happening and I got scared.

He said that when I was about four I took off all my clothes and jumped in the shower with him and at some point in the shower he felt really uncomfortable, got out of the shower and decided that he was never going to take a shower with me again, or with my little sisters. (I need to go ask him if he got an erection. I didn't think to ask that and he didn't say.) I remember being four or five, at eye level with his genitals. At the moment when he told his side of the story and reported how he felt, I really relaxed and started laughing and crying at the same time. I felt like that's really what happened.

I told him that I had another image with my first boyfriend with oral sex when he was standing up and I was experimenting with giving him head. My boyfriend got real excited and laid me back on the bed with his body and I got really scared. Both of those memories got collapsed on each other and, at that moment when my dad told me what his experience was, those two memories separated, just like that. It was really amazing. That felt really clear.

My dad said that he was deeply disturbed and deeply saddened by what I said and that his back and chest were really hurting. He kept saying, "What can I do to help?"

I said, "Just sit there, listen to me and tell me how you're feeling. This is the best thing for me." He offered to pay for everything and help me get in therapy.

After that my dad's voice on the phone sounded friendly. Two weeks after that conversation Todd and I had breakfast with my dad. He actually initiated hugging me. Prior to that, he had never hugged, and, if I hugged him, he was stiff as a board. This time my mother came in to hug me and he stepped in front of her and hugged me. I said "tighter" and he hugged me really tight. That was so good. I feel physically more comfortable around him. I told him things I would have never told him before. I even reported thoughts and sensations about giving him head as I was sitting there talking to him. Things that used to scare me because I could never say them out loud, seemed okay to say, and the thoughts, even though shocking, were really about nurturing. My mom was crying and she said, "It sounds like you're just nursing."

They stayed there and listened to this shit. I couldn't believe it! My dad's going to be 60 and my mom is 57 or 58. They have come a long way with me having conversations over the past three years.

After that first long conversation with them I got this feeling of separateness from them, like "Oh, god! They're just these people. And I am who I am, just because I am." I stopped blaming them for everything they did to "create" me.

Earlier, after my first few conversations with my mom, they gave me a car. At first I felt like they were trying to buy me off. I said I imagined that they'd get pissed off if I got a ding in the car, or wrecked it, or if I don't take care of it the way they wanted me to and asked, "Is that true?" They just sat there and laughed and said, "No, you can do whatever you want with it. It's your car you can turn around and sell it tomorrow if you want to." I thought, "Oh my God!" They were fine. They didn't care. I thought "Uh-oh, this is all me." Then I remembered that my Dad gave me a new car when I was 18.

Later when I sold that car I felt terribly guilty. So I went to my Dad and said I needed to talk about something that happened a long time ago. At first, he wouldn't look at me and I asked him several times to look at me. When he did, I said, "I appreciate you for giving me that car when I was 18. I appreciate you for everything around that car." I started sobbing and sobbing and I looked at my dad and he was smiling and he said, "Wow, I had no idea you were so attached to that car." I am so sentimental. I felt so guilty for selling it. I told him how special that gift was to me and I told him how often when I drove it, I appreciated him for it, and yet never had told him. So, I got over that appreciation as well as the resentments, and didn't feel any more guilt about selling that car. Then I appreciated my mom for giving me her car. I thanked her and I meant it and that was it.

No more guilt. No worries. Just mom and dad and me and Todd. Sitting there.

Editor's Footnote: *Cristyn's forgiveness of her parents and herself is a beautiful thing. And it was central to her reorientation to time and space based on noticing, and it could have happened sooner in her life. Her* four years of not speaking to her parents because she thought she had been sexually abused by them was partly a negative consequence from her experience with a therapist and therapy group dealing with childhood sexual abuse. The idea that she was sexually abused was suggested by the therapist asking a question, and then reinforced by the group participants interpreting that her experiences based on memories were of sexual abuse. A lot of her suffering was caused by her avoiding her parents, a decision supported by that therapist and the group.

In this case, due to Cristyn's courage in being radically honest with her parents, a therapist's mistake was finally overcome. I've known of other mistakes by psychotherapists and counselors who have held people back rather than helped them. I have coached people to correct mistakes made in interpretations by therapists, or in their misinterpretations of what therapists had said, by encouraging them to engage in honest conversations with the people they are accusing of having caused them harm.

When people make corrections in their way of thinking about people in their lives by confronting the persons they are accusing, either alone or with a mediator, and have an honest conversation about past and present memories and feelings, things get sorted out. This happens not so much because everyone figures out what really happened in the past but because everyone, in contact and conversation with each other, eventually feels their way through, rather than thinks their way around, whatever it was that they remember having happened. Radical honesty leads to a self-correcting experience of relatedness rather than a self-isolating mind jail. Corrections to mistakes of perception and categorization can be made only when secret judgments become a part of the public domain and with the people who are directly concerned. This is both more important and more reliable than interpretations by a therapist of what went on and what it meant.

Psychotherapy which attempts to handle psychological suffering by dealing with memories and feelings through work with the therapist or group alone, and doesn't include encouragement and support for confronting the real persons involved in order to clean it up, is a mistake. Period. Therapists who are afraid of their own anger, fear and hurt, often *engage in a conspiracy of avoidance with their clients, by supporting clients in avoiding confrontation with people in their families — when that confrontation is absolutely necessary; it is a great disservice to the people who work with those therapists.*

5

PAUL:
Clearing Up What Happened at that Damned Baseball Game

This is an account of a "Radically Honest"conversation I had with my parents, where I consciously intended to share information I had been withholding from them for years. Hindsight is always 20/1500, and my memory of the conversation is undoubtedly filtered through my own "story." Having written this a month after it occurred, I will remember feelings looks and words in a nice orderly way. Suspicious of my agenda and altered memories, I have tried to keep the interpretations to a minimum by sticking to what I remember I said, thought and felt.

I remember four of us sitting at a small square dining room table, my father to my left, my mother at my right and my girlfriend, Jeanine, across from me. I had a rubber band in my hand and I was stretching it back and forth. I felt tension in my chest and lower stomach. I thought about what I wanted to discuss to clear my withholds. I wanted to share some lingering childhood resent-

THE TRUTHTELLERS

ments, the circumstances of my divorce, some of my motives for leaving my father's business and moving away, and my secret sexual history. I felt tension from my stomach up to my chest and down to my anus. We were discussing childrearing.

"I give Lucas wide parameters in which he has freedom, and I keep those parameters clear and unyielding," I said, describing how I handle my four-year-old son. "When we are in a street, I make him take my hand. Elsewhere I let him run. I don't lecture him on "why" because I don't think he'll understand it." My mother said, "I was awfully hard on you kids." I looked at my mother and felt numbness in my face. I thought I wanted to respond and I didn't want to start coaching her. I said nothing.

"I yelled at you once for messing with the sprinklers in our back yard," my father said. He clasped his hands in front of his mouth, and his eyes had some moisture around the bottom. "I came outside one evening," he continued, "and turned on the sprinklers. They went every which way and I turned to you and yelled, 'Have you been messing with those sprinklers?' You crouched down and had the most afraid look on your face. I felt really bad for doing that. It was an awful thing to do to a kid your age."

"I don't even remember it," I said. I had some brief memory flashes about my brother and I constantly playing with the sprinklers and couldn't place the scene my father described. My father and I looked at each other for a moment, then he looked down and back up at me. I smiled. I felt a churning sensation in my stomach and tension in my chest. I thought about my topic list again: resentments, divorce, my father's business and sex life. I felt the tightness in my chest increase and a new constriction in my throat.

"Dad, I resent you for leaving me at that damn baseball game when I made an error!" I said, feeling heat in my neck and face and decreasing tightness in my chest. "I really resent you for that!"

We held eye contact and he nodded his head. I felt less tension in my face and chest and my face getting cooler. My hands shook slightly then stopped.

"That was at Napa High School, right?" he said, "I remember it! Do you remember your coach left that Kenny kid there as pitcher and he kept walking one batter after another? I was so pissed!"

The volume of my father's voice increased. "Around and around. I left before I told that coach what a donkey he was. I didn't want to make a scene. You were with your brother. I figured you'd make it home all right."

"I thought it was at Silverado Junior High," I responded, my voice rising, "I don't remember David being there!"

"Yeah, you and David were playing on that team," he responded. "It was Napa High and the whole team was playing terribly. I said to you when you got home, 'I'm not going to sit around and watch you guys play like that.'"

I started laughing. I felt a loosening and energy flowing up from my stomach into my head as I laughed. I felt tears in my eyes. I felt a lightness in my head. Jeanine (my mate then) was laughing and so was my father. My mother smiled.

"That's so funny," I said. "I have thought for the last eighteen years that I walked all the way from Silverado, which is about a three hour walk, when actually it was a forty minute walk from Napa High."

"It made a good story," Jeanine said, laughing some more.

I thought about when I told that story during the Course in Honesty and of the many times I had used it over the last eighteen years. I felt heat in my face. I felt foolish for having altered the story that way.

"Yeah," my father said, "That coach used to make those games so boring it used to really make me mad. That Kenny kid! Christ! Around and around! Ask David, he was there."

My father started telling baseball stories and we continued sharing and talking for the next hour. I was in my head, "checked out" going over my list of resentments, and realized I'd arranged them from least to most explosive. I thought I was a "smart coward." I refocused on the people at the table and turned to my mother.

"Mom, I resent you for telling me when I was five that if the Vietnam war was still going on that when I was 18 we'd both go to Canada."

My mother looked at me with no response then looked down at the table and said, "Well, I would have taken you to Canada."

"I know," I replied, "Saying that scared the hell out of me."…I felt heat and quivering in my chest.

"Well, Vietnam was going on and I wasn't going to let you go over there. You were my first child."

"I resent you for saying it." I noticed the sensations in my body changing again. I laughed." And I went to West Point and to Desert Storm to get back at you!"

"I know you did!" my mother said.

My father and Jeanine laughed. My mother smiled. I laughed again. We talked a bit more and I mentally checked off some resentments and reviewed the remainder of my list: divorce, my father's business and sex. My father said, "Well, I think it's a good thing to clear these things up. Hell, you'd have gone through your whole life worried about that baseball game."

We all laughed. I interpreted his tone as a signal that he was done talking for this evening. "You're right," I said, "and there are a couple of other things too…"

My father sat back in his chair. I felt energy in my chest and groin and heat in my face. I thought about having covered the first of my four topics, lingering childhood resentments, and had three to go: the circumstances of my divorce, some of my motivations for leaving my father's business and moving away, and my secret sexual history. I thought that I could quit after two and report a "respectable" Radical Honesty conversation. I looked at Jeanine, and thought that I couldn't get away with it as long as she was here.

"I'm telling you all this because I am a good storyteller. I tell my stories to hide. Like my divorce. I wanted you to think that Stephanie was at fault for the divorce. I purposely kept my mouth shut about my actions and decisions to make it look like she left me."

I stopped and was momentarily unsure of what to say. I thought about my remaining three topics. Then I thought of my divorce, felt a momentary tightening in my chest and spoke again. "I had an affair. And I asked Stephanie for the divorce. I was sleeping with Jonelle, the woman you met that night in the white car." My father's face had a look that I interpreted as questioning. My mother looked down at the table and said nothing. "You know, the pig woman," I said. I thought briefly about Jonelle, who owned a Vietnamese pot-bellied pig and one night had driven over to my parents' house with it in the passenger seat. I felt a loosening in my chest and laughed as I remembered the look on my father's face when he met the pig woman. I looked at my father, who was smiling.

"The pig woman?" he asked.

"Yeah, the pig woman." I answered. Everyone laughed.

"I felt bad," I continued, "that Lucas and Stephanie moved away. I felt guilty and did everything I could to pin the blame on her."

My father's eyes were red and my mother said nothing. He said that he was still angry that Stephanie, my ex-wife, and Lucas, my son, had moved to Indiana, and that he did blame her.

"I want to be clear that I was as much responsible for what happened as she was. In fact, at the time I was having the affair I told Stephanie that I thought I was gay. Every Wednesday I went to a support group in Berkeley for married and formerly married gay men. I went to therapists and I even dated some men. I didn't want you to know because I was afraid of your judgments of me."

"Wow, that is bad," my father said. I sat and said nothing. I felt the heaviness in my chest lighten and the tension in my neck, back and head ease. Then I felt tremendous energy in my chest, back, pelvis and arms.

"I want to acknowledge that this is easier to tell you now that Jeanine is sitting here which takes me off the 'hook.' I can make up a story about how it was a temporary problem, etc. It really happened. When it was happening, and I thought the stakes were higher, I didn't have the courage to tell you."

I looked at Jeanine and she back at me. I noticed a lightness in my chest and head, then a gentle "vibration" moving from my stomach through my chest and out to my fingertips. I continued to speak.

"I also wanted to make leaving the business and moving to Indiana seem like it was all about Lucas. That was half the story. I also wasn't happy being in business with you and I felt that I had I let you down."

I felt a tightening in my chest, heat in my face and water in my eyes. My father looked at me and he had water in his eyes and his eyes were red. He rubbed his mouth and spoke. "You didn't let me down. Not at all. I was disappointed you left and you had to go." I felt the heat leave my face and I wiped my eyes.

"I felt panicked about being in a business that I knew nothing about," I said. He said, "You wanted to know it all right up front, and you can't learn it that fast. You wanted to know everything and that takes time."

My mother looked down at the table and said, "You were mad a lot."

"Yes, I was mad," I said. "I imagined that you didn't want to grow the business and that's what I wanted to do."

I felt light in my chest and tightness in my throat. Then, suddenly I felt relaxed in my throat and started laughing. We talked for a while about telling the truth and growing up, and Jeanine talked about the conversation she had had with her parents. I remembered another withholding and spoke.

"While we are laying it all out here, on prom night my junior year of high school I had sex with Lisa and Mom found a condom wrapper in the car the next day. We had a big conversation about it and she told me not to tell you. She said it would kill you."

I laughed when I saw the look on my father's face. I interpreted it as surprise.

"Why would you say that? I would have given you the thumbs up," he said as he gave me a thumbs up. The four of us laughed as my father continued to give a thumbs up saying "Hey! Hey!"

I felt my body and I was relaxed. I checked for tension and could find none. I smiled some more and we talked about how having conversations like this livens up a trip. I asked if they had any interesting secrets to share. They said "no" and I believed them. We talked about having an honest conversation with all the children present about inheritance so there would be no misunderstandings after their deaths. They agreed this was a good idea. We all got up from the table.

"Well," my father said, "I'm glad we got that whole baseball thing cleared up!"

We all laughed. I looked at my watch and saw that it said 2:00 A.M. Five hours had elapsed. I felt relaxed and energy in my whole body. I went to bed.

Paul LaFontaine describes himself this way: "I am a Radical Honesty Practitioner at Large, Third District (provisional). My curriculum vitae includes 5 years as Liar in Residence at Mindful Universitat (Wiesbaden), three years as a Distinguished Withholding Fellow at the Catastrophic Institute, founder of Theories Anonymous (Rancho Cucamunga Branch), and a featured performer at the Master Self-Aggrandizement Storytelling Festival (held in Boise, Idaho each year).

6

SAL:
I Love You Forever
I Love You for Always
As Long As You're Living
My Son You Will Be

From the time I was little, I can't remember when I didn't want to be big enough so that I could call the shots, so that nobody could take advantage of me. I'm still trying to be big enough. Here are some of the things I remember, growing up. My dad was really an angry, angry man and he used every curse word there was available. I remember that while I was doing jobs for him— usually shoveling something, because he was in agriculture—I'd never be doing it fast enough for him. He'd snatch the shovel from me saying. "Get to the side! You're stupid! I'm gonna show you how to do this!" He'd make me watch him and never let me try again. This went on for as long as I can remember. As long as I can remember! It's only recently that I no longer want to kick his fucking ass, and tell him "Kids are not treated this way!" I remember that he cheated on my Ma. I found out about the cheating and didn't tell. I thought, "She can't find out about that because if she does they're going to get a divorce." And I needed my parents to be together, I WANTED MY FAMILY TO BE TOGETHER because that's the way a family is supposed to be. He'd make me work hard and still criticize how I did it. One day he told me to do some fucking job and when I finished it I thought I'd done it perfectly and wanted him to know this. When I went to find him I saw him chasing the maid, groping her and chasing her from behind. I didn't tell.

There were other instances where I knew he was cheating. One time he locked me in the house and in the middle of the night, when I had to pee, I went to his room and was poking at him to let me out, but he wasn't there. He had put some pillows there in the bed, and he was gone. I managed to get out the window and went to find him. I found him dancing with some girl.

But my mother ended up finding out about it. I remember that they had this fight one day. They were standing face to face and she was saying, "Tell me the truth! Tell me the truth!" She had a wire hanger and she was hitting him on his hands. The next thing I know he slapped her so hard that she fell to the ground and my dad started running. One of my sisters ran in front of him and he started fighting with her. When he reached the top of the stairs he stopped and my mother came out holding a gun. She shot him in the leg but he managed to run out.

I just couldn't fucking wait to be big enough and get out of that house. I got away and I'm still away. My whole family lives in Honduras. I sent them the Radical Honesty book. My dad read some of it and said that Brad was too fucking vulgar. He said it just like that, "Brad is too fucking vulgar." I said, "That's what I like about him. He reminds me of you." He said, "Yeah, but I don't fucking put it in books. This guy writes it in books!" I told him how important it was that I talk to him and asked him to set some time aside. So I went to see them this past Christmas.

We went off by ourselves. I was scared. But then I thought, "Shit man! I'm big now!" and so I said, "I resent you for all the times you cheated on my Mom. I resent you for the time I caught you groping the maid and I thought I couldn't tell anybody. I've been holding that all this time. I resent you for all the times you called me 'stupid'. I resent you for saying that you said I never could do things right for you. I resent you for all the times you cheated." I told him I had wanted to kick his ass ever since I was little. But the hardest part was, when I told him I loved him, I admitted that I'd become just like him, and I hated myself. I had told myself I would never be him.

He knew this was important to me and he actually took it kind of lightly. I appreciated him for that because I realized how I made a big deal of this whole thing—a huge deal. It's what I did when I was little, and it was so big for me because I had kept it secret for so long. He just said he was sorry. He thought he had done the best that he knew how to do, that he wasn't perfect and that he had done some things he wasn't proud of. He said that the worst thing he had done was that he hadn't been close to me or to any of the kids and he wished he could take that back. That made me feel pretty good that he said that.

I don't remember a time when I ever hugged my dad. I hugged him. I hugged him and it felt good. I hugged him and I kissed him and he said he liked that. I liked that. I realized for the first time that I didn't have to play "Bottom Dog" any more which had always been the mechanics of our relationship.

I noticed that it came up for me again when I was going to quit my job, start training in Radical Honesty and not make money for a year. He said, "Well, shit man, you can't do that. That's crazy, you know?" I just let him go on about it and I still have to talk to him about that some more. I notice that now I separate myself from what he thinks vs. what I'm thinking and doing. And I also notice that it's okay with me if we differ and I don't have to change his mind. I like that. That's freedom. That's true freedom, not to think that he has to be pleased with it or in accordance with whatever I do in my life. That was my completion with my Dad.

With my Mom it was easier because we've always been very, very connected. What I had to do was to tell her that I wasn't going to pick sides any more. I wasn't going to try to save her from the marriage that she had picked and always complained about. She stayed in that relationship and it's the way she wanted it and I understood that. I said I could love them both the same and I didn't have to pick sides and I didn't have to treat her better than my Dad. I created a lot of pain for myself trying to pick sides all the time. She said that she understood and she said that I was doing the same thing my sister Patty had done a few years back by telling everyone everything. And she cried.

Then, that night I brought out a fairy tale book. It's called *Love You Forever*. I recruited everybody in the family to come listen and to act out the parts — and we have lots of people in the family. There are seven kids and their grandchildren and all kinds of family. The book starts with a little baby being born. The mother's holding him and she's singing, "I love you forever. I love you for always. As long as you're living, my son you will be." And he grows up and goes through the teenage years and he's got purple hair and he's doing weird stuff and making a mess in the house and she sings, "I love you forever. I love you for always. And as long as you're living, my son you will be."

The son grows up and moves out of the house. They show a picture where the mother is driving in the middle of the night with a big ladder on the car. She's sneaking up through the window, sneaking onto his bed, as old as he is, and she's singing to him, while he's asleep. She says, "I love you forever. I love you for always. And as long as you're living, my son you will be." The son grows older and one night he gets a call that his mother is very ill. She's on her deathbed. He goes to her and picks her up from the bed and rocks her singing, "I love you forever. I love you for always. And as long as you're living, my Mom you will be." In the next picture they show the grown son going up the stairs in his own house and he stops for a long while, then runs over to his little baby daughter and he sings, "I love you forever. I love you for always. As long as you're living, my daughter you'll be." We all cried. Afterwards there was a lot of laughter. It was fun.

I realized then that I don't have to pay the price of being away from my family any more. I can be connected to them, and yeah, I created it all the way that it was up until now. Now my brother is coming to live with me. And when my mother comes to visit she can visit both of us. He loved the idea, and I love it.

My whole family loves me. It's just amazing to me because for so long I tried as hard as I could to get away from them. For me to be able to put that little play together... I just had to ask and every-one wanted to be a part of it. That was pretty amazing. It amazed me that I could create that kind of difference in the family, that I could create any kind of difference.

Sal Quiroz is a Radical Honesty Trainer Candidate. He lives in Florida. He will be taking Radical Honesty trainings to South America. He is currently in a relationship with Amy, whose story comes next.

1

AMY:
Getting Over It
With My Dad

I called my dad and told him I was coming to show him my "life story" videotape from the Course in Honesty. He didn't get what I was talking about, and he didn't care, but he was glad I was coming because I never visit. My brother told me I was going to kill him by doing this because my dad has a weak heart.

I think it's important for y'all to know I didn't really know how to get to my Dad's house. I packed all the camping gear just in case I didn't want to stay there, but Sal and I did end up staying there. At times during the weekend I wanted to run off to the springs and camp out to avoid the task at hand. Sal supported me in going to see my dad. He helped me make that whole trip happen, and for that I am grateful.

I was in my head a lot of the time. I really had myself freaked out—heels dug in the earth and pretty uptight. I was pretty much unwilling to set up any time schedule for showing the video to my Dad. That was misery, and I was acting like a victim. It wasn't pretty, until finally I gave up and gave in. But by this time my dad and his wife were enrolled in my fear of THE VIDEO!!

My dad and I sat out on the porch swing and he said he was afraid of getting his feelings hurt. I told him I imagined it hurts his feelings worse when I don't send him Father's Day cards or cards for any other holiday. I said that I was willing to give up my victim story here, and that I wanted to re-create our relationship. That's when he said he didn't see anything wrong with our relationship. Then Sal put his hand on my dad's shoulder and looked him in the eyes and said "Mr. Fitzgerald, do you realize that your daughter didn't even know where you live? Let me tell you, I know exactly where my father lives." FUCK! My heart hit the ground and I looked at my dad. His eyes changed and softened; he looked sweet and said "O.K. let's do it."

Sal took the girls [my daughters] into town, then Dad and I put my life story in and sat on his bed; I noticed my breathing was quick and shallow, so I kept trying to take deep breaths. Then, I noticed the way my dad looked. He was really into it. He was talking to the screen saying things like, "Oh, I don't remember that...hmm, that must have been a blackout." He was animated so I loosened up and enjoyed watching him. I imagined he was getting to know me, and I loved all the attention. He made sad sounds about my dog dying and I liked that he seemed to care. When I talked about my black boyfriend, and all the affairs I'd had, my body was tense. His face changed and I was back in my head in fear.

As soon as the video ended we went out to the kitchen to sit at the table, but the repair man who was working on the house in saying he needed my dad to go for a part. I imagine my dad was pretty happy to haul ass. So when he left I was backed up, scared and frustrated and his wife gave me some feedback. She said that I looked troubled and that I've always looked that way to her. She said that she supported me in doing whatever I needed to do. That was great, but we didn't talk about it in detail or very directly.

Sal came back and asked, "So how was it? Well, I can tell that you haven't had breakthrough just by looking at you." I was angry and frustrated and still scared. I decided, in that moment, to start telling the truth about resenting my dad for everything I resented him for—like when he pointed at me as he spoke. I also resented Linda (Dad's wife) and I still was not getting to any appreciation.

My dad wanted to take me for a drive to show me the small town he lives in. I thought, " It's going to be a long ride home to Ft. Lauderdale if I leave it like this." So, as we drove by the bay I saw a pier and asked him to stop. We sat at the end of the pier and I explained that I was afraid to resent him and, again, he was enrolled in my fear—but it was still nice to sit out there with him. I liked the attention...hmmm... anybody see a pattern for prolonging the work?

By the time we got back home I was ready. I was tired of being afraid. I wasn't going to go back home with all this shit! We got into the story about how, when he was 30, he had the world by the balls and then his wife said she was pregnant AGAIN! I resented him (pretty strongly) for telling that story at family get-togethers. I told him my interpretation of that story, and how all my life I've imagined I was an accident and unwanted by my dad, so "fuck you for not loving me" has always been my theme. That has been the underlying message in all my communication with my dad as long as I can remember. Well, he was shocked said that I'd gotten it all wrong. I imagined that he was frustrated by the look in his eyes and the way he was using his hands for emphasis. He gave me examples of how he had always wanted me, by saying how he really wanted me to have his nickname "Toby," but my mom wouldn't hear of it. Then he resented me right back for not telling him sooner. He kept saying, "I can't believe you've walked around with this your whole life. Does your mother know you feel this way?" He started to look sad. And then, in that moment, when my eyes were focused, my hearing acute—I heard him say he loved me. It was one of the first times if not the first time I've heard it and felt it at the same connected moment—that he loves me. Sal and Linda were cheering in the background and they sounded far away. I was in this moment with my dad. Like I've never been. We cried. We hugged. And I let him in.

Amy is a hairdresser and the mother of two girls and is an intimate relationship with Sal. They live in Florida.

8

KATHRYN:
Curiosity, Courage & Contact

The following are missives I sent via e-mail to friends and relatives from June through February, relating what happened and how I reacted during the course of the search for my biological parents. My parents tried for five years to have children and adopted me when I was born. They conceived my brother, Jeff, a couple of months later. I've always known I was adopted and had no other information. My mom told me, before she died, that she understood that I might some day want to search for my birth parents. Dad has also always been incredibly enthusiastic whenever I've considered doing so. But it was not until I got really interested in knowing the truth, about everything, win, lose or draw—and had the support of a group of people who loved knowing the truth—that I actually did something.

Last January, I discovered the name of the adoption agency that placed me. It was behind a photo in my baby album. I received confirmation on March 31, that the agency would initiate a search.

June 18:

On Tuesday, June 16, I heard from the caseworker searching for my biological parents. She called to introduce herself and give me the non-identifying information she had up front. Ohmygoshohmygoshohmygoshohmygoshohmygoshohmygosh! I made myself not cry so I wouldn't miss anything. Here's part of what she told me:

Mother: 17 years old; 5'6-1/2"; dirty blonde hair; gray eyes; freckles across cheeks and nose, tans well; Swedish descent; strict Catholic upbringing, now Agnostic. Enjoys painting (studying art in school), horseback riding, swimming, playing the piano, and ballet dancing.

Father: 18 years old; 5'9'; "dark brown hair with straight lines;" dark hazel eyes; Irish descent; "a leader"; plays bass in a band; has built an engine; has built a kayak; family in the military. Enjoys canoeing/kayaking, horseback riding, swimming, and reading. I'm stunned to have information suddenly. It's been 34 years. The caseworker also put my birth date and mother's maiden name in a search network and GOT A HIT!!!!!!!!!!! She sent a certified letter the next day to the woman and said she would call me when she got a response. ohmygoshohmygosh. I've been all jittery inside!!!

June 24:

So. The caseworker, Janice, called again, Tuesday, June 23, at 8:20 p.m. and told me my birth mother had called her in response to the certified letter. I sat down. She told Janice that I'd been conceived in love and she would like to make contact with me. I started crying. "that she'd like to meet me." … "that her husband knew and was all for it." … "that she has two children"– I have a half-sister 31 years old and a half-brother 26 years old. Oh my, oh my, oh my. She will tell them about me after we meet. Janice asked me if I still wanted her to search for my father; I said yes. Janice said she has to write a report to the Virginia Department of Social Services and receive their disposition to release my name, telephone number, and address to my birth mother and hers to me. This will take about two and a half weeks all told. I'm welcome to call Janice anytime to see where we are in the process. She won't write the report until she's exhausted all leads on my father–the report is the end of the search. NOW I'm kinda freaking out. I'm going to meet the woman who gave birth to me. And maybe my half siblings. Ohmygosh... Dad's psyched for me.

August 12:

These last two weeks I have been getting strung out: tight stomach, nausea, eating chocolate and drinking Coca Cola, not sleeping, generally freaking out about waiting for the caseworker to call with a name, a place, anything. Well, she did.

So, yesterday at 6 P.M. the caseworker called to tell me that the woman's name is "Sammi Winter." She lives (drum roll) in a suburb of Washington, D.C. GASP! Twenty-five minutes away! Oh my god. The caseworker said she (Sammi, for lack of a better handle, such as birth mother, mom, mother...) would be home after 8 p.m. and would be calling me at my home number. I'm house sitting, so I left a message on my machine with the number and that I'd be in after 9 P.M. My friend, Christine, and I proceeded to go to dinner, drink a little sake, and TRY to chill.

At 9:05, after making sure Sammi had not left a message on my machine, I called her. A man answered the phone. I said, "Hi. I'm looking for Sammi Winter." He replied, "Okay." I ventured, "I'm Kathryn Lyle." He said, "She's been waiting for you." Ohmygoshohmygosh. GOOSEBUMPS!! I could imagine the smile on his face by his tone of voice and I just melted! She began, "Hello."

I said, "Hello," and lacking a mind interrupting me, "How are you?"

She replied, "Frantic," and laughed, "How are you?"

I said, "Nervous, anxious, and excited." We both laughed. Forty-five minutes later, we'd agreed to meet on Friday at 11 a.m. here in Washington.

We agreed not to meet at a restaurant because she said she'd be crying. I told her, fine, because I would be too. Awesome. The conversation covered nuggets and wisps of information. All amazing to me. She's bringing photos of my father (GOOD GRACIOUS!) whom she hasn't seen since several months after my birth — she went to Europe after graduating from high school.

I'm so excited! Last night and every time I relate our conversation anew (usually telling more than the outline above) adrenaline just flows through my veins, I hold my head up, I smile hugely, move my hands a lot, feel fluttering in my midsection and chest; I am SO PSYCHED!!!!

I called Dad immediately, told him everything I could that she and I had talked about, and he is also completely excited. He was even reluctant to get off of the phone with me. He's coming over Friday afternoon after she's left. Unbelievable. Wonderful. Marvelous. Yesssss! I am thrilled!

August 16:

Yessss! At 10:45 a.m. Friday, August 14, I opened the front door and exchanged stares with my birth mother, Sammi Winter. She's tall, 5'7-1/2" and very slim; long pony tail, with blond highlights; vivid blue eyes and defined facial bones; tan. We were both wearing black pants, blue shirts, silver jewelry...Hmmm.

She showed me photos of my father taken a month after my birth — he was 17. The pictures are small, black and white, and I resemble him around the mouth, my smile. He's handsome and very young. I resemble her most in profile and around the eyes. We both can do the Spock eyebrow maneuver. She gets a giggle out of this. We talked about our lives and went to meet her husband downtown for lunch.

Antonio Dinero III (Deet)": he's disarming, charming with shining blue eyes and a wonderful open smile; very happy this reunion has taken place. Both her children are excited to meet me and I, them. Her daughter, "Angie," lives in Colorado and their son, "Antonio IV," lives in Montana (my brother and sister, as Sammi calls them).

When we arrived back home, my dad was waiting, so they got to meet and talk for a couple of hours. Dad thinks she's all good. He's got a good sense about people. I spent the next afternoon and night at the Dinero's place. They have a big old Victorian house, some parts fixed up, some not. Twelve-foot-deep porch, no A/C, one phone, bathtubs with buckets to rinse, 11 bedrooms, all sitting on several acres — my kind of relaxed old-fashioned atmosphere. Many books. A little Twilight Zone feeling; am I dreaming? That's my DNA walking ahead of me. Geeeez.

Sammi introduced me to a couple of people, "This is my daughter, Kathryn." Incredible. Goose bumps. I've been smiling a lot since Friday. Open feeling in my chest and rib cage. Sense of calm and satisfaction overall. Happy. Sammi's told me I'm to get a passport ASAP, and I'm to come out to their home anytime, often and unannounced. I have expanded my family by several. Nice. I've talked to my brother Jeff, Uncle Fred, Uncle Bert and Aunt Priss and my cousins Frank and Julie, lots of clients and friends and every one's pleased and supportive. I am blessed!

November 15:

I've talked to both my half-brother and half-sister (hereon referred to as my brother and sister), my Uncle Abe, and been introduced as "This is my daughter, Kathryn." and "This is my niece, Kathryn." UNBELIEVABLE!!!!!!!

I've spent the night at Mom's house several times now and we are going to Montana for Thanksgiving to meet my brother and his family. My sister came east from Colorado on October 15th with my 15-month old nephew and we had great conversations, laughs, and hugs! I was supposed to go to NYC to meet and stay with my grandmother last weekend and was too sick to do it. I'll see her in Montana. CAN YOU EVEN?????!!!!! Here's me, diving into the deep end, and finding the water fine.

Actually, I'm in a tailspin. I didn't foresee how much of an impact this would all have on my life, my past, and my future. I have come to understand a whole new appreciation and gratitude for my adopted mother. She was a brilliant, attractive woman and a great parent; thoughtful, protective and though not cuddly I always knew she loved me even when I felt like I hated her. And even then I loved and respected her. She did the best she knew how and I thank her for it now. More when I return from Montana.

February:

Sammi says, the older she gets, the more she wants solitude. She really does read all the time, and when I visit then, she, Dan and I sit around in front of the fireplace and talk for hours. I notice I want her to be more social; want her to meet my friends, to come into town more often. I love her any way she cares to be. I've gotten more than I ever hoped for or imagined and I'm grateful for her and the rest of my now larger family.

THEN...

I searched for my bio-dad's name on the AOL White Pages and came up with two hits!!!! One in Alexandria, Virginia, and one in New York City. I called the caseworker and asked if she had also found these men and did they perhaps decline or were the wrong ones? She repeated what she'd told me months ago, which didn't help much. Sammi and I joked about doing drive-by's; or setting up an easel outside the New York address and seeing if I recognized anyone. She said that the one in Virginia had to be his dad, the General, and we simply did nothing.

July 1:

Sammi got out of her own way and called (Ret.) General Denholm. She told him who she was; he remembered and they had a conversation anyway. He said Charles was working and living in New York, and (I'm abridging the story a lot here) said she could call him at work. She then left for Montana for two weeks without telling anyone.

Longer story short, I agonized, stressed, and procrastinated about writing a letter to him. July 22, I wrote and rewrote it several times and on July 23 I put it in the mail with a photograph.

July 28:

HE CALLED! Left me a message saying how wonderful to get my letter, how I look just like my mother, that he wants to meet me and left his phone numbers. Ohmygosh…I called my dad, called Sammi, went to swing class, told several folks — because of course I could not contain myself (imagine!), and came home around 9 P.M. to call him.

We talked for 30 minutes; and he was wonderful, laughing, excited — his wife was laughing in the background! He has a son who's a year younger than I, and a daughter who is 31 and recently married! Their mother and he have been divorced for 26 years and though he's been married to his current wife for only four years, they've been together for over 24 years. He shuttled down to D.C. a week later and I just spent last weekend in New York City with him and his wife! We e-mail almost daily and talk on the phone every other week. We're completely in love! Definitely a chemical bond there. He's handsome, athletic, funny, down to earth, a great cook … what's not to like?

So. Full circle. I've come full circle. And I'm home.

9

NANCY:
A Death in the Family

I grew up in Oklahoma, in the country, in a family that was stern and conventional. Our parents did not show much affection and punishment was swift and sure. My father was what I assumed was the typical dad, stern, authoritarian, and strict about us kids following his rules. He made the rules and they were to be followed to the letter of the law. My Mom was a homemaker, and took a passive role to my father. She raised the kids and he punished them.

There were six of us, born approximately two years apart, and alternating boys and girls. The first son was Martin, and the first girl, Wilma. As the oldest boy and girl, they had authority over the rest of us, which they wielded with glee and which we resisted just as gleefully. The second son was Gordon, and the second daughter, Patricia, or Patty, as she preferred to be called. I learned much later in life that after Patty was born my Mom tried to get her tubes tied, and the doctor refused to do so without her husband's consent and she was so mad she refused to do that. So, my Dad had a vasectomy, which apparently didn't work, as two years later my brother James was born, and two years later, I was born. I remember my Dad telling me I was born on a fence post, that a crow deposited me, or that I came after the mailman. I think he said similar things to my brother Jimmy. I never knew what he was talking about until I was grown, and realized he was intimating that I was not his child.

As the two youngest kids, Jimmy and I hung out more with each other and did lots of things together when we were small. I remember one summer Mom giving us each a bucket to play with. I was probably 3 and Jimmy was 5. We went searching for horny toads, lizards, bugs, snakes and other treasures to put in our buckets. All of us kids loved to play outside. I think it was safer for us outside.

When I was five we moved to another town in Oklahoma, Canton, where we stayed until I graduated from high school. The summer after we moved I started first grade. School was okay, but the summers were the best. We still played outside as often as possible. There were fields of plum bushes to make forts in, and eat from. There was an orchard where we would sit in the trees and pick fruit on hot summer days, eating it slowly. It seemed the summers stretched forever.

I remember one summer I was out walking in the fields with Jimmy. I was barefoot, which was not uncommon around the yard. We were out in the field behind the house though, and as we were walking home we ran into a sticker patch. I stepped into them, and immediately got a foot full of stickers. I remember crying, and stopping because if I stepped in any direction I would get more stickers in my feet. I was stuck. Jimmy had shoes on, and came to stand in front of me, and picked me up piggyback and carried me out of the sticker patch. I will never forget that.

When I was eight, and Jimmy was ten, he went hunting with our thirteen year old brother Gordon on New Years Day, 1960. Gordon had just gotten a twenty-two rifle for Christmas. I remember telling them "good luck" as they walked off, and then feeling embarrassed for saying it. We did not say affectionate things and it was unfamiliar to me to blurt this out. I always remembered later thinking if I had not said this, Jimmy would not be dead.

A couple of hours later, someone heard Gordon off in the distance yelling for help. I remember panic and yelling, and lots of activity. The rest is a blur to me. I seem to remember Gordon running up to the house. He was covered with blood. His shirt and pants were wet and red. An accident had happened. Jimmy was carrying the rifle, and tripped and shot himself in the head. Gordon had picked him up and tried to carry him all the way home, but could not make it. He laid him down by the road, and ran the rest of the way to the house, yelling for help.

I remember Mom gathering all of us kids in the kitchen and telling us to pray for Jimmy. I felt embarrassed because I did not know what to say, and certainly did not feel up to the task of asking for a favor from God. So we all sat there, silent, uncomfortable. I tried to pray and also not to cry. I remember the awkward silence and not knowing what to do. I would glance up every once in a while to see if I was doing what everyone else was doing. Most had their eyes closed, or were just looking at the table.

Finally, my Dad came back and we learned that Jimmy was dead. He was DOA at the hospital. I don't remember him coming home or who told us or where we were or what we did. I only knew that our prayers did not work. The pieces I remember from that time are scattered and uncomfortable for me to remember. People came by and brought food. The doorbell rang a lot. I remember starting to hide whenever I heard it ring. I was not used to people coming by the house so much. I was not sure what was going on, but I knew everyone was quiet and unavailable.

One evening a week or two later, my oldest sister took me outside. It was still early January. I must have been asking about where Jimmy was because she wanted to tell me something about him. We sat outside and looked up at the stars. She told me that Jimmy was now a star up there, and that is where I would see him. I remember I did feel some comfort from knowing that, at least I knew where he was.

One other indelible memory I have of that time was of my brother, Gordon. I saw him lying on the lower bunk bed in the room he had shared with Jimmy. He was lying on his back, arms folded back and his hands under his head. His knees were up, with one foot rested on the other knee. He was staring up at the bunk where Jimmy used to sleep, and he seemed to stay that way for a long time. I remember looking in at him, thinking someone should go to him, and help him. Someone should talk to him. I knew he blamed himself. I also knew that Dad blamed him, and maybe Mom too. It was the rule in our house that the eldest were responsible for the youngest kids. Gordon was the oldest on the hunting trip. Therefore, even if nothing was said, he was responsible for Jimmy. We all knew it. And, Jimmy was dead.

If we kids thought our parents did not get along before this, it was even worse afterwards. The silent treatment between them became an everyday occurrence.

There was a new rule in our house after Jimmy died. It was that we were never to speak Jimmy's name in the house again. I don't think the rule was ever said out loud, but we knew it. I guess I understood or learned the logic that if something is painful, don't talk about it, or it will make it worse. I remember accidentally breaking the rule several years later. I was maybe ten years old. I was home, talking about someone in my class whose name was Jimmy; as soon as I said his name, everyone got quiet. No one looked at me or said anything, but I shut up too. I remember thinking I should have known better than to say his name. I had brought up something painful which was not acceptable.

I didn't realize until after I had grown up that this rule and the agreement of the family never to talk about him or the accident that killed him prevented me from ever grieving Jimmy's death. I do know that whenever I told anyone about my brother who had died where we were young, I would get tearful and tense, my throat would get tight, and I would end up choking back words and emotions. Consequently, I did not talk about it much. After all, it happened long ago, we had put in the past, and so it did not affect me much anymore. At least, so my mind told me.

When I told my life story at the eight day Course in Honesty workshop, I told this story, and cried so much I could hardly talk. I could not give many details or answer many questions about how Jimmy died or how we dealt with his death. I mentioned that no one really knew what happened when Jimmy was shot, because we never talked about him or his dying after it happened.

Somehow in the public telling of this I also realized for the first time that there was an unspoken insinuation in our family that maybe Jimmy did not shoot himself. Maybe Gordon had accidentally shot him, and no one had wanted to ask about that. We did not talk about what actually happened, so why talk about what might have happened? Was there a cover up because it would have been unbearable for Gordon to deal with? Or, more likely, would it have been unbearable for the family to deal with? More importantly, none of us had ever talked to Gordon about what it was like being there with Jimmy when he died. We were not supposed to talk about it, and we were still not talking about it. I saw what a huge secret this was, and what a huge price we were all paying because we had never talked about Jimmy or shared our grief. We did not even know what had really happened to Jimmy or to Gordon.

When I got home from the eight day, I called Gordon and asked him to come over for supper. I was scared, my throat was tight, and my stomach had butterflies.

I had never asked him an intimate question about Jimmy before. I wondered if he might get defensive and angry. We had both ended up living in New Mexico, far away from the family and Oklahoma and we both liked it that way. We did not see much of each other though, maybe once or twice a year. I attributed this to the fact that we were not a close family, although I had always liked Gordon more than anyone else in the family besides Jimmy. We were the only two who had emotionally left the family and felt like we did it for our own survival. We were the only two who did not regularly go back to visit the other sisters and brother. I certainly did not enjoy visiting them much. Gordon didn't either. We did it because we felt obligated to do so.

Before supper I told Gordon about the eight-day workshop. I told him I realized I had never asked him what had happened when Jimmy was shot and died. I said I remember there was a family taboo against talking about Jimmy. It was hard for me to talk about Jimmy and bring up the topic. I asked Gordon what had happened that day. He told me the story.

He said he was so looking forward to taking Jimmy hunting because he wanted to be the big brother to Jimmy that Martin had never been to Gordon. He was proud of being the older brother, showing the younger brother the ropes about hunting. He said Jimmy had wanted to carry the rifle, and so Gordon let him carry it. They had just crossed through a barbed wire fence and were still hiking in the fields. Jimmy was walking behind Gordon when Gordon heard the gun go off. He looked back, and Jimmy was lying on his back, eyes open and staring at the sky. Blood was oozing from a hole in his right temple. Gordon said he felt sick, he knew Jimmy was hurt bad. He called his name but Jimmy did not respond. Gordon picked him up and put him over his shoulder and carried him as far as he could, yelling for help.

I learned things I had not known before. He was too far away from the house for anyone to hear him. He couldn't carry Jimmy any further, and so laid him beside the road. He ran the rest of the way home, yelling for help. As Gordon got closer to the house, someone heard him yelling. Dad ran out and Gordon told him what had happened and they and Mom got in the car and drove to where Gordon had left Jimmy. They laid Jimmy on Mom's lap in the front seat and Gordon sat in the back while Dad drove to the doctor's house in our small town. The doctor could not do anything except offer a towel for the blood coming from Jimmy's head, and call the ambulance. When the ambulance arrived, Dad went with Jimmy in the ambulance. Mom and Gordon drove home. Gordon said he did not remember any conversations going into town or coming home. It was when they got home that Mom had us gather in the kitchen to pray for Jimmy.

I was crying as Gordon told me this story. It was the first time I had heard anyone describe that day. I recalled my own memories as he told his. I imagined how scared he must have been when he saw Jimmy lying there. Nothing could change what had happened. I remember often as a kid wishing and thinking "if only." If only I had not said "good luck." I am sure Gordon thought of many "if onlys" too. If only Gordon had not gotten the .22 for Christmas. If only they had not gone hunting. If only Gordon had not let him carry the rifle. If only Jimmy had not tripped.

I looked at Gordon as he told the story. He looked away most of the time. Gordon's eyes were big and wet but he did not cry. I asked him if he had ever cried about Jimmy and he said yes, he had, a lot. He also told me that Jimmy had come to him in a dream many years ago, and had told Gordon that it was okay, that he was okay, and that his death was not Gordon's fault. I cried about that too, and am crying as I write this.

Gordon also remembered that we were not allowed to talk about Jimmy or mention his name again after he died. Gordon said it was as if Jimmy had never existed in our family after he died. Since the day of the accident, Gordon said no one had ever asked him what happened to Jimmy or talked to him about the accident again. This was the first time someone in the family asked him what his experience of that day was.

Gordon and I still have a lot of talking to do. About Jimmy. About our family. About our relationship. I like Gordon even more now than I ever did. The more I get to know him, the more I see him as a wonderful human being and a wonderful male human being.

Once the family rule was in place not to talk about Jimmy or what had happened the day he died, I never questioned or challenged that rule. Not until the workshop, when Brad asked, "what really happened that day?" I realized I did have the right not only to ask the question but to find out from everyone what really happened and what their memories were. I was definitely scared about challenging that rule, but I was willing to do it anyway. I also knew there would probably be consequences to challenging that rule. I imagined that my siblings would not want to talk about something that had been supposedly completed years ago. I could hear them already. "Why would you want to bring that up?" "Why don't you just let it rest like the rest of us do?" I am learning that I have the right to ask questions for my own information. I have the right to find out what really happened. I have the right to know even if no one else wants to know. I have the right to want to know even when I am told I don't have the right to know.

Gordon and I are both learning to be less defensive about what we have done and how we come across to other people. We are learning to be accountable for our behavior, and not for the assessments others may have about our behavior. After I started talking to Gordon about things I had been avoiding talking about, we started to see more of each other. We even started to include my husband, Jim, in our conversations about these previously private and secret matters about our dead brother Jimmy.

Since becoming familiar with the tenets of Radical Honesty, the illusions we all have that we are in control, and the lack of actual control we have about everything we do, I have often wondered about my getting married. I lost my best friend Jimmy when I was eight years old. By the time I was fifteen years old, I was sure that I would never get married. I remember clearly, making a bet with my junior high basketball coach. His name was Mr. Clinton. He said I would be one of the first girls to get married after I got out of high school. I took him up on that bet. I knew I would not get married. I would not go through what my parents had gone through. I would not hate the person I was married to. Since that was likely, I just decided not to marry anyone. Why would I want to end up hating the person I was with yet staying together for some archaic reason?

Well, I won the bet. I was still single at age thirty-five; then I met my future husband, Jim Cebak. Only eight months later I was married to him. I still wonder if I was waiting to meet someone who reminded me of the brother I had lost long ago and whose name was James. I still use the nickname of Jimmy as a term of endearment for my husband. And I wonder if I did not really want to break the family rule of not speaking the name of Jimmy by bringing a Jimmy into the family. Who knows? Who cares? The point is that I do have a best friend again whose name is Jimmy. And, like my brother, he would gladly carry me across a sticker patch if I ran into one.

I enjoy spending time with Gordon now. He has been funny for as long as I can remember. I don't know if this talent emerged after Jimmy died as a defense against the tremendous pain of his death, or if he was always witty and quick with a quip. Either way, he is a very funny person, and lots of fun to be around. Gordon did the Radical Honesty eight-day workshop in Albuquerque after our conversation. I imagine we both have a long way to go. We are still talking.

Nancy Darbro, Ph.D., is a nurse, drug abuse counselor, psychotherapist, heads a statewide drug abuse treatment program and is a Radical Honesty Trainer. She and her husband, Jim Cebuk, who is a Radical Honesty Corporate Trainer, live in Bernalillo, New Mexico.

10 PAIGE:
Christ, This Is Fun

S hortly after leaving Virginia we found out my Dad's cancer
had spread and he was terminal. He died New Year's Day.
We're convinced he was holding out so Mom could use him
as a deduction on her '98 taxes. The whole dying process was
exhausting, stressful and sad. Mom was amazing. Every dying person should experience a caregiver as devoted and loving. She also
paid for every one of the trips home for us kids and our spouses so
we could spend as much time with Dad as possible without financial worry. She did all this without creating an atmosphere of guilt.
We had plenty of time to say good-bye, share stories and appreciations, and process resentments. We all planned the non-traditional,
non-religious memorial service while Dad was still alert enough to
tell us what he wanted. Mom asked my brother and me to prepare
a brief memorial for the service.

When I learned that Dad was terminal I noticed that my resentments were easier to remember and worried about writing a
memorial. As we went through the next three months together and

I spent time with Mom and Dad really remembering what it was like growing up, it was amazing how much I found myself appreciating. By the time the service rolled around, I wrote my memorial in less than an hour. I gave this memorial at his service and it brought the house down. It also provided me with closure. I now smile proudly about the way we lived as a family and the way we dealt with death as a family. This is what I said:

"I'm Paige Cox-Risteen, Dad's daughter. I wrote a letter to my dad to share with you but before I read it, I'd like to point out how ironic it is that, if Dad were still alive, he wouldn't attend. He hated these things.

Dad, I used to say, I was afraid of you until I was twelve and then figured out you were kidding. Now however, I know you weren't kidding. You were just preparing us for an unfair world in the only way you knew. You were scary then. Tall, with a loud voice, and strict. You had rules for everything. You were consistent though, and we always knew what to expect. Even our neighbors knew what to expect.

When the whistle blew, the Cox kids came running. When the streetlights came on, the Cox kids better be getting home. Still, our house was the one the kids all felt welcome to come to and play basketball and kick-the-can. And you were the only dad who came out to play, whatever the game. You saved us all from numerous injuries when you made us start playing flag football instead of tackle, as we were killing each other in the field. Then you provided the old socks to use as flags.

You enjoyed us more the older we got, and we enjoyed you more. You became less scary and more fun. I remember playing lots of cards, especially cribbage, and riding bikes to family tennis matches. You and I against Tim and Mom followed by a bike ride to the Dairy Queen for an ice cream pig out. Dilly bars for us and a cherry malt for Mom.

You prepared us for our first family ski vacation with the Cox Family version of Boot Camp: an almost daily 2-mile twelve-minute run around the church parking lot. (The same parking lot where you later taught us how to drive a stick shift in reverse. Reverse, because you thought that at that speed, we were less likely to damage the car, ourselves, and most importantly, you.) After our morning runs, we'd partake in another one of Dad's Grand Schemes for Physical Fitness: dinner at breakfast. We'd have pork chops, hash browns and Mom's homemade apple-sauce. I sliced the potatoes for hash browns and made the orange juice. That's still about the extent of my cooking capabilities. Andy has to handle the rest.

Andy's first family gathering involved an afternoon of peeling, quartering and slicing apples for Mom's homemade applesauce. It was then that you introduced him to one of the Cox Family Motto's: "Christ, this is fun." If you were here now, I feel certain you'd say it. So, I'll do it for you: Christ this is fun.

You rarely missed our track, cross-country or swim meets, always proudly wearing those dorkey, "I'm Tim and Paige's Dad" T-shirts and sucking lollipops through Tim's record breaking high jump marathons.

You didn't inherit Grandpa's tinkering and mechanical apti-tudes. I remember you and Tim trying to put together a set of lawn chairs. After several hours, several beers and lots of giggling, you presented your finished product: backwards lawn chairs. You claimed the directions were faulty! But whether or not it was the directions, the beer or a missing mechanical gene, after several more hours of beer and giggling the two of you figured it out and enjoyed the story as much as the chairs.

You hated house and yard work, preferring to play golf and tennis. You were able to avoid a lot of what you didn't like doing. First, you had Mom. Like other women of that time, she did every-thing. Then, Tim used to say you had him so you could get out of doing your share of chores. You were able to do just that with your creative disciplinary system. You'd ground Tim for whatever limit he was pushing at the moment, then, with one day of work equal to one day off his grounding, you conned Tim into single-handedly painting a house, installing a chain link fence, cleaning the gutters and completing all your lawn work. You got your work done, got to play tennis and golf and kept your rowdy son off the streets.

You kept me off the streets by taking your "dateless daughter" to every sporting event and movie that Mom didn't want to go to. We chose more carefully after sitting together in red-faced silence watching Jane Fonda have oral sex with Jon Voight in *Coming Home*.

You coaxed me into hitting the tennis ball with you several nights a week. "After all," you'd say, "this could be the last time". You fought your disease (he had MS) so valiantly for so long, I don't think either of us ever believed there'd really be a last time.

I'll miss you, Dad, though I'll carry you with me always because I am much of what I appreciate and resent about you. Your competitive spirit, your sense of justice and fair play, your integrity, your dark, dark, sense of humor, your coloring, your build-including those masculine hands we share, and mostly, your great love of life, your friends and your family. I hope that in my life I am loved as gently and as fully by my friends and my family as you were by yours.

You once told me that in your dreams, you walk. In mine, you're running, preparing those out-of-shape legs, because when I left you last, I said, "I'll see you next time". You asked me if I'd look for you. I said I would. You asked if I'd be sure to find you. I will find you, Dad, and we'll go hit that tennis ball one more time. I love you.

Now, one more time, the Cox Family Motto; "Christ, this is fun!"

Eighty people said, "Christ, this is fun" with me and we all laughed. Then we went home and had a party and toasted Dad.

It was wonderful to have an opportunity to get more clear on my feelings about growing up and my relationships with my Mom and Dad. I felt incredibly articulate and joyful at and after my Dad's service and I appreciate you (Brad) because I imagine you played a part in that piece of my growing up through the workshop and the conversations we had after the workshop. I feel that I've been blessed with the opportunity to say good-bye to my Dad without guilt or remorse and with a remarkable amount of joy in celebration of the life we had together.

Paige Risteen-Cox is a corporate executive and a Human Relations trainer.

11

EVE:
Breaking the Shackles
Around My Heart

I want you to read a letter I sent to the members of my string quartet, about a month ago, so I am forwarding it to you. But first I want you to know that my personal, internal "odyssey" began when I picked up your book, *Radical Honesty*, while I was in Hawaii. I read it in one day. I finally stopped underlining, because every word made sense to me. Then I called your office, and registered for my first "Course in Honesty" workshop, presented by you, in March of 1999. That started my intense relationship with Radical Honesty. As you and I both know, at times the going got very, very tough.

Remember when I did not get up or out of my trailer for several days? And when I was volunteering in the office and did not bother to show up at the office? I was busy. I was hollering like a needy infant in my trailer, camped on your beautiful land. I spent hours desperately screaming, and feeling the same sensations I think I may have experienced in reality, after my birth, when I was left alone way too long, screaming at the top of my lungs. My parents made a joke of it: "With such a loud voice she may be destined to become a Wagner Opera singer." They didn't realize I was screaming, "Help, HELP, HELLLPPP, I need you! I NEED YOU! Please, come to me, please hold me, HOLD ME, SMILE AT ME, HOLD ME ... KISS ME." These were the words I hollered then, and now, at 58 years old, in my trailer, I was yelling same words while rubbing my lips hard and incessantly with my right hand, experiencing to the depths the very need of my lips to touch skin.

When I was born, in Nazi-occupied Holland, babies were raised on a strict feeding regimen; I had to wait for the clock. Weeks went by like that described by my mom in her journal. Today we know, thanks to the appearance of that wonderful book, *A General Theory of Love*, to which you refer so often, that a week-old infant does not have the physical reserves to bridge a period of acute hunger and discomfort. The desperation I felt in my trailer was not unlike dying. I was helplessly screaming from inside my mind "I do not know how to survive, I need your help!" Yet at the same time, I remember how I feared "others" and could not ask for help. I did not know what help would look like.

Up until those days alone in that trailer, through my life I had used my compensatory mechanisms to continue to feel separate, with a big smile on my face and lots of "can-do" energy. There was such irony in that. But it was an old, familiar comfort zone, feeling isolated and lonely, at the same time, I made sure I was keeping my distance from others by using my facade.

You came knocking on my trailer door, and told me any time I wanted to "talk" you were available. I remember how I answered, "I do not know what to say. I have no words. I do not know what is going on. I am in the process of learning to tolerate whatever the hell is happening to me." Your car drove away...and I went back to desperate crying...many, many hours of it. The sun rose outside my window on the left, and the sun set outside my window on the right, and I witnessed the splendor of the star filled skies, and the shooting meteors, over those beautiful mountains of the Shenandoah Valley.

I believe that you helped prepare me, through everything you said, wrote and taught, to descend one more time into what seemed like a bottomless pit of extreme suffering. Raven encouraged me just to experience my experience, no right and no wrong about it, and she would massage me, with essential oils. The truth was that my survival-mask was beginning to crack...and I did not know how or who to be without it. Very hesitatingly, and certainly not overnight, the genuine, authentic me began to surface.

My love goes out to you Brad, and deep appreciation for your own courage to speak your truths. You have a permanent place in my heart...and so does Radical Honesty. That is where this letter to my friends in the quartet came from:

"In Celebration of my Father"
Gainesville, January 2002

Dear Michael, Ned and Bob,

Yesterday, after I had left Miami's manmade madness behind me on the Turnpike, not far from the Miami International University exit, I accidentally found myself in the turn-off lane at a badly lit construction site, on the ramp to Highway 27 North, which I remembered was also a good way to drive to Gainesville, so I took it.

In the watery dawn, while passing many trees with large, bloom like white shapes nestled on their branches, alternating with brown-black blooms — which after closer inspection appeared to be birds, still asleep in their "sleeping trees," I was touched by the beauty of life — the self-evidence with which the Ibis and other birds slept so peacefully on their branches — the self-evidence with which the sun rose — the self-evidence with which the blue heron, startled by the noise of the oncoming freight train, flew across the road, almost directly over the hood of my car.

I began to imagine the three of you, and I wanted to share this experience of beauty with you, and I realized at the same time, I would like to share it also with my father. I remembered and re-experienced the love I had felt for him up until I was not quite 5, in 1949, when he had to leave for Indonesia. He was gone for 6 months, which I experienced as forever. That all returned to me in full force. I remembered what I used to have and that in 1949 "I left" my daddy (my pappy) and began to belong to the emotional domain of my mother.

I turned off NPR, and observed quietly as this Florida land-scape passed by the windows of my car, graced by shards of fog, and pastel colors, created by the rising sun and light traffic some-how reminiscent of the 1950s. I felt and saw all at once—the reeds waving in the wind, the wind itself, the sugar cane, orange groves, lakes... I cried. I smiled. I gushed. I began to feel the presence of all three of you...and my father.

My father was born in 1908, in Bogor, Netherlands Indies, and had a beautiful soul...which I FELT until I was 5, and finally dared to reacknowledge, but only intellectually, the last summer of his life in 1992. I loyally catered to him then, and told him to ask me for whatever he needed. He and I knew he had begun to die, and he and I were able to talk about that. Images from that time recur: The day he was so terribly constipated, he called me from the bath-room, lying on the floor, next to the bath tub...too tired to get up, with that insistent, maddeningly urgent need to have a bowel movement, hoping it would happen any minute. He told me this secret, begging me NOT TO TELL MOMMY...just like my sister Rinske and I had asked of each other when we were growing up, whenever something important or painful was happening to us. (I alerted the home-visiting nurse, who came to give him an enema, etc.) My mother was at the piano, upstairs, in her own house, obliv-ious to what was happening that afternoon, which was typical of how she had been all our lives. She continued to despise him for his progressive physical "weakening," yet "served" him loyally, all the while showing her irritation.

We all had failed each other at loving. We suffered behind our masks, while playing our roles. He and I did so consciously — my sister and my mother, I believe, almost completely unconsciously.

He was a very loyal man, not untypical of his generation. He was also very gifted and very, very sensitive. He was an avid black and white photographer. I grew up with a panoramic view of the glacier of the Matterhorn, hanging in the windowless W.C. in seven square 12" x 12" panels. I used to count them. They were developed in his makeshift "darkroom," the same windowless bathroom with bath, shower and sink, where I used to watch him shave and shower, until we, the children and he, were no longer supposed to be there nude together in the early morning rush to get ready for work and school.

He had been a hotshot tennis player, playing club tournaments. He rode a Harley Davidson, when he was courting my mother. He studied at the university in Rotterdam. He was an exceptional pianist...dreaming of making music his career... meeting and marrying my mom instead. She studied piano at the Conservatory. He PLAYED the piano ONLY ONCE in my entire lifetime. I only heard him play a quick arpeggio, while walking past the opened piano. But I saw him turning pages for my mother, during the chamber music sessions in their house after he had retired. He was thrilled by the music making in his own home and the camaraderie with all those excellent amateurs, passionate music makers, from all sorts of walks of life.

When he was 72 and my daughter was born, he came to visit in Gainesville. When he saw how I mothered my own child, and when he was present during our rehearsals of the Gainesville Chamber Orchestra, and when he witnessed how I taught the many students that came to my house, he told me how much he enjoyed observing the way I did all these things. He admired how

I interacted so personably with "the kids" and adult students—how I was able to make the music sing, help them make the music sing. He said, "What you do is so different from Mommy who plays so heartlessly—is so cerebral". But, somehow it was too late. I could not let his words sink in and touch me. I failed to get over how we had all failed each other at loving.

Yesterday, in that glorious morning on Highway 27, my feelings of love for him returned very powerfully. I experienced with sadness the fact of him not knowing the three of you. Not seeing your integrity. Not seeing how you enjoy his daughter! Not seeing how worthy you and I are of each other. I imagined him talking photography and music with you, Ned. I imagined him talking tennis, music, Philippines/Indonesia, colonial history and finance with you, Bob... I imagined him talking Zen, and music with you, Michael and Ned...

I remember that later on, when I attended the week-long silent Zen-retreat in Miami, which was at the time of my father's birthday and also the date of his death, a most delicious (Indonesian) peanut "sateh-sauce" was served for dinner once, and I was in tears. I sat and cried over the "sateh-sauce" with big, heaving sobs at the dinner table. I stayed in my chair, amidst the other participants, accepting what "was," knowing it would pass. My father COULD have been awakened, COULD have dropped his mask. Instead, he told me about my great-uncle George Gonggrijp's play "Asoka", about the Buddhist ruler, and he gathered some Eastern artifacts, some now in my house. That was the best he could do.

He never spoke about his mother, who died when he was 17. Losing her was too tender, I think. While he and I were sitting next to his dying cousin, in whose home he had lived after his mother's death, and where he had been made to feel extremely unwelcome by his uncle, he talked about his life to me. I heard his pain. He had drunk too much Jenever. For years it had seemed to me that he lived for the Jenever-cocktail hour. I had insisted I drive him to the nursing home, to sit with him and his dying cousin. We left Katie, my daughter, with my mom, as her consolation prize. I heard more about him than I had ever known. BUT his speech was clouded by alcohol; so I listened to him only with loyalty, and with my mind. I did not allow myself to FEEL WITH HIM...from my heart. He reminded me, right then and there, that when he died, he wanted to be buried in the family graveyard where his mother was buried. He told me how he often had gone there on his bike, during his lunch break, when he was still working in The Hague. I asked him where it was. He told me. Now I know what a beautiful place it is because we brought him there. I finally went there with him, walking behind his coffin with my mom, my sister, her husband, my niece, and lots of flowers from our garden, on a watery, cloudy day.

In the 1950's he began to buy vinyl records. He would come home with music he knew of, but did not intimately know. He and my mother had played all the "standard-literature" for four-handed piano Brahms, Beethoven, Mozart, Haydn, Schubert symphonies, quartets, and, they always went to concerts. During his childhood his mother took him to the opera, concerts, and the theater in The Hague. He was her "escort." His father had remained in Indonesia, where she "could not tolerate the climate," as it was said. I believe she left because their marriage did not work out. Several times in the 1950s my father and I listened to the Chinese Baritone Bass Yei Kwei Szei sing the Aria's of the Czar in Moussorgsky's opera "Boris Godunov." I remember him getting extremely animated, verbal and excited about comparing the orchestration abilities of Stravinsky, Moussorgsky and Ravel. My mother, already irritated about his Jenever drinking, was yelling that he was playing the music too loud! "Please mind the neighbors!" "Isn't it about time to go to bed?"

During those record listening evenings I felt very ill at ease with the emotions my father showed and experienced, amplified by Jenever. So again, I kept my emotional distance, even as we were both similarly moved by the music. He would often get very teary. I pretended not to notice.

After his retirement, my father would sit in his "den," overlooking the garden with a thick hedge of roses climbing up against a separating partition. I had helped build that, between our yard and the neighbor's. (And it was faithfully cared for by my mother, who spent many hours working in the garden). During the late 70's and 80's, he would sit there planning and be occupied with his stock portfolio. He NEVER talked about money, and he looked down on us three women, for being "un-business-like." I believe this topic had to remain his own, private domain, where he felt successful, superior over us, safe and in control, in a "man's" world.

When he died in November, 1992, he left my mother a house and close to four million guilders. I was STUNNED. I had no idea he had acquired that much. Large sums went to the Dutch IRS...twice. When my mother died 16 months later, my sister and I paid the inheritance tax a second time. I guess he arranged for everything, including his prophecy about us being "unbusinesslike" to be fulfilled.

Something happened while I was driving yesterday. The shackles I learned to hold so tightly around my heart were broken further and are now beginning to fall away. You, Ned and Bob, demonstrated this summer and fall with our music-making, what it looks like to devote yourselves to something, in order to satisfy yourselves, for your own pleasure. You develop your own potential, because you want to. You showed me actually what it takes to commit yourself to something...."just because;" you do what you do with a certain amount of discipline. You consider carefully what you spend your time on. Recently, Bob, I saw your grace on the tennis-court, the high level of your developed skills, your candor to Rob Kanzer when he visited; and in St. Pete, during our Da Ponte Quartet worship, when we were throwing the tennis ball back and forth, I saw such pleasure on both of your faces. I EXPERIENCED my own love of running, playing tennis and chasing a ball—and music. I began to love and recognize my own potential; I began to love to develop my own potential further. I began to love...me and you...and my father...my sister...life...this grand experiment in being.

I want to celebrate the 10th anniversary year of my father's death by inviting the three of you to go with me to see and hear *Boris Godunov,* by Moussorgsky, performed by the Miami Grand Opera in March. I know Bob likes opera, and we have already discussed going. I do not know if you, Ned and Michael, do. Since it will be costly I want you to honestly tell me if seeing that opera would not really be a treat for you. You are the three men I have learned from most during this summer and fall and I would very much like to share Moussorgsky's incredible opera with you. I will surely feel emotion when I hear this music I listened to with my father, and have not listened to since.

From my opened heart,

Eveline d'Angremond

Today, I am thoroughly enjoying translating Clark Accord's historical novel The Queen of Paramaribo. *The English-language filming of that book will happen in Paramaribo, Surinam, and I hope to be involved with the English script development. I also hope to translate Brad's* Honest to God *with Neale Donald Walsh into Dutch. My violin playing is better than it has ever been. I live in the here and now, at ease without my mask, and with great compassion for me, you, humanity and mother earth. A new intimate friendship is developing with a favorite man. I believe many wonderful things will come out of this new clarity of speaking, feeling and thinking!*

12 JONATHAN:
This Person in Front of Me Happens To Be Mom

Thanks to Kevin, Michael S. and Ken from the Course in Honesty in the World 2003, for asking me about what happened when I had another try at a completion conversation with my mother just after New Year's Day. Here's my story.

Since I did the 8 day Course in Honesty a year ago in October I've had a number of conversations with my mother about my childhood, my perspective on it, and her perspective on it. I'd expressed a little bit of anger, cried a bit, and Mom and I have gotten a lot closer; but I definitely wasn't complete. Sometimes I'd feel a volcanic, burning, roiling sensation in my chest and belly that I interpreted as anger and I'd fill pages and pages in my journal with all sorts of "I hate her" crap. Mom and I talked about this on a few occasions, we both knew there was stuff going on for me and that I hadn't forgiven her for what she did and did not do when I was young. She'd also made it clear that she was ready to talk when I was; and I found that really helpful in not being quite so afraid of the consequences of what might happen if I expressed whatever I felt.

When I headed down to Virginia for the 5-day over New Year's I was expecting to leave from there to drive cross country to go to Esalen. I felt pretty warm towards Mom, and she towards me, and she told me that she was missing me terribly before I even left. I knew I was leaving incomplete; my story was that competion could wait awhile, and I'd be doing assorted personal work over the next few months. Maybe when I came back we'd talk more, or something like that — great avoidance behavior. At the 5-day Course in Honesty in the World, we did an exercise answering questions taken from Greg Levoy's book, *Callings*. One of the questions was about goals and actions to anchor our calling in the world, and the only thing I could come up with was doing whatever was necessary to get complete with Mom. To my surprise, nothing came forth about becoming enlightened, meditating, attending workshops, writing, teaching, counseling, none of that stuff came up. Just getting complete. Finishing unfinished business. That was it.

Then Ken and I had a long, late night conversation about blame, fear and relationships that gave me some direction. Kevin (a.k.a. Dr. Dream) and I did some dream work; and Julia told me she was really turned off by my little boy act. Further conversations and experiences over the week also helped, particularly seeing Michael E. and Roscoe in the "informal" hot seat work. An insight I had was that people couldn't help but be honest, no matter what. Either they express their honesty in some indirect, passive way (like my supposedly helpful judgments that are often expressions of anger), or they are direct about it. I found this really liberating, as sadness, anger, etc. in me is going to come out in one way or another, so why not get those feelings over with and move onto something else?

The afternoon of New Year's Eve I had a resentment of Anne (who was assisting Brad in the workshop) In resenting her I kept on giving up and could not quite express it. "What's the use?" kept on going through my head. "I don't want to resent you, I want you to love me" also went through my head in a whiny little voice, and I expressed that in different ways, verbally and non-verbally. And I didn't get really loud at all; the people who were in hearing range said I was being wimpy. I agreed—I'm really good at being resigned and then subtly spiteful. So, with all that, I decided to rearrange my plans and go back to Maine and have a conversation where I'd forgive my mother. Complete forgiveness would've been great, I thought, but I was hoping for something like 50-60%. I also knew that I probably couldn't do this very well on my own, that my own patterns would get in the way. So I asked Anne (who lives about 45 minutes from my mom) if she would facilitate, and she agreed.

On New Year's Day, Anne and I flew up to Boston and her partner, Rob, picked us up and brought us to her place in Kittery. It's a nice house with cozy rooms and all sorts of interesting antiques. The next day, Anne and I drove up to Kennebunkport. Anne and my mom spent some time getting acquainted, and Anne explained the process and intention of a mediated radically honest conversation to her while I took care of some errands. Then we sat down, my mom and I across from one another, with Anne facilitating. I started out really slow—swallowing my words, smiling, giggling. Sometimes my voice would go up and I'd get this shy expression on my face as I did my little boy act. I was really aware of holding my hands together on my lap. I had thoughts like "I don't really have to do this, we can get along fine." At the same time I really appreciated Mom for being there and being willing to participate and I told her that I loved her. Anne at one point compared me to others in the group I had criticized for wimpiness and rationalization and I agreed. I now think of this as "premature compassion"—trying to get to the good stuff without acknowledging or completing the anger and sadness.

Eventually, I was able to start expressing some resentments. There were three main areas of resentments, plus some resentments in the moment. One scene was Mom and Dad arguing before getting divorced, the second was the events around my birth and

Mom not telling anybody that she was pregnant until she got married; and the last was for the times when my mom came in my room to talk with me after the divorce, when I was really withdrawn. I resented Mom for being loud when she was arguing, for telling my sister and me to be quiet, for not coming upstairs to check up on us after they finished arguing, for sometimes storming out of the house during an argument, for slamming the door when she did, for telling my sister and me to not slam the door, for getting involved with my stepfather (they had an affair for several years before Mom & Dad got divorced), for having him come over in the middle of the night and then leave, for not telling us anything about it, for coming into my room, for not staying longer and drawing me out, for having me (that was a big one), for not telling anyone about me, for lying to my father about being pregnant, for how she looked, for how she moved around, for sitting still—all that.

In expressing all these resentments I wanted to speak quietly, venomously, so she would "get it" from how bitter and mean I sounded, then I wouldn't have to say anything more. Anne encouraged me to repeat things, to get louder, to actually express how angry I was rather than just imply it. Often I'd get a little louder and then I'd stop resenting with a kind of sigh and have some sort of "what's the use?" thought. I started hating that sigh. The first time I really got into resenting her I started crying and my mom did too, and then she got up and came over to me. Anne and I both asked her to go back and I lost the thread of whatever I was experiencing. Later on, I resented her for coming over to me. She resented me for some of my resentments around her pregnancy with me. That was it.

I had a really hard time getting loud, just too many internal injunctions/principles. I was silent a lot, thoughts running around in my head, wanting to say them, only my throat and mouth weren't complying. Eventually I did start yelling from my belly and not just from my throat. I noticed when I did that my shoulders started moving more as well, like more of my body was getting into the act.

Other times I hollered, and a couple of times my breathing got chaotic, almost sob-like. I was glad to have that experience. (I've done exercises trying to get in to chaotic breathing in order to relax the conscious hold on myself and always found it difficult.) At times I found trying to explain things to my mom didn't work, and I'd end up more disconnected than before. Just staying with "I resent you for... and I appreciate you for"... seemed to work a lot better. I sobbed a little a couple of times, and laughed occasionally. Sometimes it felt like avoidance behavior, other times I laughed at such ironies as yelling at my mom for yelling, hollering at her for telling us to be quiet, stuff like that.

A couple of hours into all this Mom and I were still sitting across from one another and suddenly my perception of her changed. She went from being "Mom" to a person sitting in front of me who happened to be my mother. And I loved her and we had a history together. Instead of seeing "Mom" with all the stories , trauma and BS, I saw a person and realized "Oh, hey, that's Mom." I resented her some more after that and getting loud wasn't such a big deal and neither was saying the really painful stuff or the stuff that I imagined was really petty or would be really hurtful to her. I appreciated Mom for some more things, like not coming up the stairs, for being with my stepfather, for being there with me, for having me (a bit), for how she looked, and for being my mom. And then I told her I loved her, and I felt really warm doing that.

We ended up hugging one another for a long time. I cried more, really relaxing into crying like I'd never really done. At this point crying was okay, somehow, when previously it hadn't been. I got her sweater wet with my tears and desperately tried to keep all my snot from dripping out. I think I succeeded in that. Then I really appreciated Anne for being there. So did Mom. Anne appreciated Mom and me, and there were lots of appreciations all around.

That night I slept at the house; and the next day when my mom and stepfather drove me to the station, we had a good conversation, which we all enjoyed. Saying good-bye, Mom and I both felt really connected and complete—she told me that she wasn't sad or missing me in the way that she had when I'd left at Christmas. In the days since, I've felt really warm and loving towards her and a few times I've picked up my cell phone and called to say that. Now whenever I talk or write about this, I get a buzz, feeling really high, and I have a big smile on my face. I feel really expansive, and I want/wish/hope everyone could feel this way all the time. If this is what forgiveness feels like, I want more of it. Never having done this before, I don't know how complete I really am with my mom, but I would guess 75% or more.

Since then I've noticed a few changes. One is that my voice has gotten deeper on average—it still goes into higher registers when I'm playing the little boy to get attention or when I'm nervous, but mostly it's lower. Another change is that I'm more content just sitting here, not doing anything. In the past I've felt compelled to make the most of every moment, always doing something. My mind still generates all sorts of thoughts, but I don't seem to take them as seriously (most of the time). I'm also less nervous when I contemplate whatever I might do in the future (I've spent many many hours being anxious over that). Having done the thing I was most scared to do, everything else doesn't matter so much. However, I still hesitate to consider a completion conversation with my dad.

Sometimes I feel that by having that conversation with Mom I did something really good for myself, and that means that I can do other good things, too, that I don't have to be stuck. I feel really blessed/fortunate/lucky to have a mother who is willing to participate in my own healing and growth. I'm also a lot more aware of the two ways that I most commonly avoid being contactful—my "little boy" story, and my "being right" story. And mostly I'm really happy and grateful to be here, alive, in this body, and I like that a lot.

Jonathan Drummey is a Radical Honesty Trainer Candidate, a hell of a catch for someone looking for a good husband.

PART TWO

SOURCING THINGS AT THE SETTLEMENT

Current Family Relations
—Husbands, Wives, Kids, Ex's

"A living body is not a fixed thing but a flowing event, like a flame or a whirlpool: the shape alone is stable ... We are temporarily identifiable wiggles in a stream that enters us in the form of light heat, air, water, milk ... It goes out as gas and excrement—and also as semen, babies, talk, politics, war, poetry, and music."

— Alan Watts

"You must have chaos within you to give birth to a dancing star."

—Friedrich Nietzche

What To Do When
Things Work Out

Charles Wilson was having an affair, and not for the first time. He had actually had many of them, maybe about twenty altogether, since he had married fifteen years ago. Several of them were with other men. Most were with women he met at work, or on occasional trips away from home for work. He loved sex and had a lot of it.

He came to see me in psychotherapy because he was miserable. He was having conflict at home and at work. His kids were miserable. His wife was miserable. His parents were miserable. He couldn't sleep. He was tired all the time. He was depressed. I told him to stop lying and start telling the truth, that it was his secrets that were ruining his life.

Suddenly, one day, he told his wife the truth about something. Initially, he told her only some of the truth but not all of it. Then he told her about having had sex with someone else. She was hurt and furious to start with, but then wanted to know more details. Each time they talked he hadn't quite said it all, and when he revealed what he had held back when he told her the first time, she got really really mad. With the help of more coaching for both of them, he described, in detail, the number of times he had seen his lovers, what, specifically, he had done with them and how he felt during the liaisons. This occurred over about a two-week period of intense conversation between him and his wife, including several two-hour mediated sessions with me.

His wife went from hurt and furious to furious and hurt. She cursed him, threw a chair at him, made him move out of the bedroom, and told him to prepare to move out of the house and made plans for them to separate. She cried and was hurt over and over again and expressed a lot of resentments. He cried, got mad, was hurt, felt guilty, apologized, accused, took it back, took back the apology, apologized again. He was confronted by other people in a couples' group who hated his guts. He was yelled at and cursed by his most recent secret lover for breaking up their affair and violating their secret. She was empathized with, accused, blamed, supported and pitied in a feminist "throw the bastard out!" group of her own.

Ultimately, he told the whole truth not only to his wife, but also to members of their couples' group and then to selected friends of theirs as well. Both of them lived through a lot of fury, hurt and fear in the weeks following his coming clean. They were coached by me and by other friends who simply held constant for them the goal of being explicit and clear about what they felt, what they thought and what they had done. The objective was the same for both of them: to reach a place of clarity, in order to make a decision about separating or staying together, not based on immediate emotional reactions to the past. That is, they wanted to get to a place where both of them could sit in a room, looking at each other, and neither one would have an ax to grind, or a demand to be met, or a feeling unexpressed. Then they would have a conversation. The conversation would be held on the other side of having completely experienced their way through all of their reactions based on actually knowing the truth about what had happened.

At one point in the process, Charles began looking for another place to live. But they both agreed that before he actually moved out, the kids (9 and 11) would be told that their parents were thinking of separating and given a chance to work through their feelings, while their father was still in the house. They told the children and had honest conversations with them about the decision they were trying to make. In the few weeks they were doing that, his wife forgave him further. Then, when they had forgiven each other completely, together they made the choice to continue living together. They also made some new agreements about how they would do that. They shared their agreements with the group and continued in the group for support in recreating their marriage. He was no longer depressed. He could sleep. He wasn't tired all the time anymore. Conflict at work slowly went away.

That his wife was able to forgive him for screwing around and for lying about it was miracle enough, but what followed was even more amazing. There was great joy and renewal in the whole family. The kids, who were eventually told the whole story, started doing better in school and feeling happier. Mom was happier and her business grew. The family weathered the whole crisis together. The perspective and the conversation and the closeness that developed out of that renewal continues to this day, many years later.

If this sounds like a fairy tale to you, join the crowd. People have a hard time believing this story and a lot of stories like it. What's more, this brief description of the beginning of renewal barely represents an even more unbelievable, bigger story, which continues on. This family is still together and better off than ever. Not only have the relationships between the parents and children improved, the relationships the parents have with their own parents are better. It was as though some kind of positive virus began to spread, and it moved up and down and across members of the extended family.

Several years later, when the grandfather died of cancer, the whole quality of ongoing honest sharing in the whole family allowed the husband, who was the original transgressor, to love and care for his parents in a way that would not have been possible before the discovery of the value of telling the truth. He was no longer depressed and unable to sleep, no longer tired, or unhappy at work, as had been the case prior to his telling the truth. And his relationship to his whole family and everyone he knew, began to blossom. His work life improved; he got a series of promotions; he was elected to office in his union and was given merit awards and raises. He became a mediator for conflicts within his organization. His wife's business boomed and grew, primarily because of the quality and then expanded because of the quality of her contact and authenticity with people. They became the center of a group of friends who performed music and sang together and helped each other with the ongoing exigencies of life. The virus spread among their friends is still spreading to other families because of this couple's work.

That story is about people who stayed together and were able to continue raising their children while living in the same house. But it doesn't make a bit of difference whether you keep living together or not; you have to do the same psychological work anyway. When you have children, whether you keep living in the same house with each other as primary partners or not, you have to get over your grudges, your hurt and your resentment, your romanticized view of how things could have been, should have been, and get over it, get over the tragic tales of being betrayed, jilted, abused, and stepped on, or whatever other bullshit revisionist tale your mind makes up about who is to blame. Before being free to do a halfway decent job of caring for your kids, or move in to another, or several other, intimate relationships, you have to do this clearing work of forgiveness.

I could go on, but I will shut up. That is enough to introduce these upcoming, equally unbelievable, stories. Suffice it to say that all of us are trying to have our lives serve as a warning to others. That warning is: Don't take so long to get over things! Stop avoiding, hiding, withholding! Face up to people and work things through, or your life will run its course without you having lived!

Part Two: Settling Things at the Source, is about honesty between couples who are the source of families of their own. These people are sharing honestly with us to help further the spread of the Radical Honesty virus, even though it seems to be something most of us have been inoculated against by the way we were raised and educated. Vulnerability to this lucky virus improves once we have experienced enough of the life of lying, and begin to question the validity of strong cultural taboos against living out loud. The healing virus takes hold when people have risked, in some circumstance or other, telling the truth, even though their mind was shouting at them not to.

13

AVERILL:
Completing What Was Incomplete With My Ex-Husband

A week after finishing my first eight-day Radical Honesty course, I asked my ex-husband to watch my life story videotape, which had been made at the workshop. I told him I was ready to answer all of the questions I had been unwilling to answer fourteen years ago when we divorced. He agreed to view the tape that night and to talk the next day.

Upon directions from Brad, it was my intention to get complete with my ex-husband by telling him, face-to-face, that fifteen years earlier I'd had a brief sexual encounter, gotten pregnant and had an abortion, and that I had hidden it all from him throughout the remainder of our marriage and our divorce. I was very scared. Actually, scared doesn't begin to describe my experience. I was terrified, shaking like a shaved poodle. From the time I'd had the abortion to the time of my Radical Honesty workshop, I'd kept this secret entirely to myself, causing me many sleepless nights, sadness and silent grief. For the first time since I'd met my ex-husband, twenty-five years earlier, I was about to do something new: tell the complete truth to the best of my ability.

I had hoped the hour-long tape of my whole life story as I had told it to the group at the workshop, and the goodwill I'd tried to create in recent years would help him to understand and soften to me. But when I arrived at his door he opened it with a scowl on his face and threw the videotape against the stone fireplace behind him. "Doesn't that about cover it all?" he growled. I told him I still needed to say some things to him. He walked ahead of me into the living room. As we sat down to begin our conversation, I was already beginning to feel the familiar signs of withdrawal, dry mouth, clammy hands, constricted breathing, itchy scalp, and the overriding impulse to crash through the double pane plate glass window in order to get some air and be with my furry friends, the squirrels.

He said to me, "I watched your tape about the affair and the abortion and about how you can relate to other men, but not me. Why in the Hell can't you relate to me?" His voice was rising, "Why can't you communicate with me?" I felt small and exposed. I felt like I was four years old again, and about to get my whipping.

My inclination was to, as the song says, "Go to Carolina in my mind." But I had been to Brad's Radical Honesty workshop and knew that my habit of withdrawal was not connected to the divorce or the abortion. The real fear was in my head, created by me to cover a deeply grooved unwillingness to communicate within myself. I was doing it to myself. He was there, but I had created him there.

In the eight-day workshops I'd been in, Brad had taught us to breathe deeply and to connect with our bodily sensations during the absolute pinnacle of our crisis. I'd seen him talk people through this while they were on what's called the "Hot Seat," and witnessed some remarkable emotional breakthroughs. So, I had confidence in the process, even if I didn't have confidence in myself. Because I promised myself no matter what came up, I would not run this time, I began a rhythm of slow deep breathes while I asked myself, "What's going on in your body?" After a few deep breaths, I noticed a tightness in my throat and a familiar lump there that was a signal to me of tears not far behind; but I felt a little calmer. The noticing helped me switch my focus long enough to stay in the room. No running this time. No crashing through the plate glass, no drinking to cover my feelings, no lying to cover my shame. It was all there in its rawness and clarity: two people, who at one time were married, but who'd never learned to tell each other the truth, tripping over twenty-five years of lies and emotional withholding. For one of the first times ever, I was able to stay in his presence, feel my pain, his pain, see his anger and not run.

I was able, one shaky second at a time, to keep my seat; we talked for a while longer. He told me he resented me for keeping the kids to a rigid schedule of visitation—MY schedule of visitation. He told me that all the other resentments were gone except for the one I'd just given him, because he lost sleep the night before after watching my videotape.

I told him I resented him for threatening me at the time of our separation with taking the kids. I told him I did still have resentments towards him. I told him I resented him for not trying harder to make a marriage with me. He asked me what he could have done better. I told him he was always right and that I wish he would have tried to be a little more fun. He admitted that he wasn't much fun. He still isn't much fun.

I told him I appreciate him for being a stable presence in our childrens' lives and for making efforts in recent years to include me in holiday gatherings at his home and for listening to my Radical Honesty. I told him I was sorry for my part in the failure of our marriage. I cried. He got less angry. When I left we weren't closer, he was still angry, but I felt better inside. My worst secret was out to the person I'd spent all these years hiding it from. I felt wrung out, but free. I no longer feel deep shame in his presence. I am a little closer to me, if not to him.

Three years after my completion with my ex-husband, there is still no great emotional depth to our relationship, AND we are on better terms than we have ever been. Now that we have lightened up on our incredibly unrealistic expectations of each other, we seem to smile more when we are together. Even though we are not "a couple," we meet with our children about twice a month for dinner and a movie. We take care of one another when we are in need, and we call ourselves a family.

...Leading to Completion With My Mother

Three years and two more eight-day workshops later, I sat at the life story videotaping portion of the workshop. As I was being filmed, I was describing my efforts to engage my family of origin in a Radically Honest conversation. My two sisters and mother were still unwilling to talk about Radical Honesty with me, and my sisters had refused to go to therapy with me. In particular I wanted to express some debilitating resentments I held for my mother concerning the violence and alcoholism that pervaded my childhood, but she refused to talk about the past.

Brad said, "There are still a few things you haven't tried with your family." I responded with, "The only way I'd go to Boston is if Brad comes with me." He said, "Let's go Tuesday." The people in the room told me my face drained instantly of color and my eyes glazed over with the look one might expect to see on someone who'd just been informed they were to be shot at sunrise. Although I'd been asking for years, doing a completion with my mother was something I felt was not within my grasp in this lifetime. Accepting "No" for an answer was familiar, asserting myself was not. Brad said, "You do not need her permission to talk to her." What a concept. I paused for about five seconds and then heard someone who sounded like me say, "OK."

The decision was made. Brad had offered to help me do this completion three years earlier but now I was ready. Like Janice Joplin sang, "Freedom's just another word for nothing left to lose." I didn't see how things could get worse and this gave me the freedom to take the risk to make things better.

We flew from Washington D. C. on Tuesday, rented a car, and drove to her house. As I pulled the key out of the ignition, I bent my head across the steering wheel and said to Brad in a barely audible voice "I'm so scared." He said, "Let's go, they've had you buffaloed long enough."

My mother opened the door with a smile. She is shrinking now, smaller than I remembered her and completely white-headed. Just seeing her brought tears to my eyes and shook my resolve to tell her my resentments. I felt my small child, longing for Mom, rise in my throat, and the pain of wanting her affection coupled with knowing I was about to say the most difficult words of my life to her, began to send me into my old immobilization routine.

She wasn't expecting Brad. I had told Brad that we would never get in to see her if my sisters knew I was bringing him. They knew who he was from books I'd sent them. But my mother was polite. After I introduced Brad, she said, "You're not with that Radical Honesty are you?" Brad said, in his sweetest Southern drawl, "Yes ma'am I am, I wrote the book." Quickly, he told her he'd come with me to help me get over some things from my past. He asked her if she was willing to hear what I had to say so that I could put the past behind me. To my surprise she said she would. She and my sister and Brad and I sat as directed at the dining room table, while my brother-in-law went to the kitchen to make us some tea.

Brad didn't waste any time. He said, "Ave, go ahead and tell your mother what you resent her for." I told her all I wanted was to be able to sit next to her without feeling afraid.

And now, even now as I write this, tears are falling and I feel as if I am about to vomit. I said, "I resent you for telling me you were going to beat me within an inch of my life and for making me and

Marie lie in the bed. I resent you for ripping a leg off the kitchen table and beating me unconscious." She listened until I finished, then leaned sharply towards me with the angry face I'd always been so scared of and said, "You deserved it." Suddenly I did feel my anger and I leaned toward her and shouted, "You should have been arrested for what you did to me! I resent you for all the times you put your fist in my face! I resent you for the way you're looking at me right now! I resent you for telling me you had no use for me!" She told me the beatings taught me a lesson. I told her, yes, they did; they taught me to stay the Hell away from her, and from anyone else who might love me.

It went on for four-and-a-half-hours. I told her that I appreciated her for sitting and listening to my resentments. I told her this was the first time in a very long time that I'd felt love from her. After some prodding by my sister, my mother apologized for what she had done, and I hugged her and appreciated her for apologizing. But the words that meant the most to me were spoken in an undertone while Brad was talking to my sister Faith. She said, "I could have killed you and I'm glad I didn't." I've been waiting to hear those words for forty years.

There were some loud resentments exchanged with my younger sister and I told her I was sorry for several mean things I'd done to her when we were children. She wasn't expecting that and she ran from the room in tears. My older sister was unwilling to communicate with me. I regret this even today, but I imagine her fear of and unfamiliarity with Radical Honesty put her into an unresourceful emotional state. Brad asked her if she was willing to meet with me at a time of her choosing. She said she would.

The next morning I had breakfast alone with my mother. I burst into tears over the pancakes and told her that I was sorry for my part in all the hostilities and in particular for withholding my love from her. She forgave me and I told her I would make a trip back to see her before the year is out.

A few days later I got a message on my answering machine from my sister Faith. She said she wanted me to come back to Boston to go to therapy with her at last.

My mother still says she doesn't want anything to do with Radical Honesty but at the same time admits that good things came from the encounter.

Completion Update:

Progress with my family of origin has been slow. Due to our two-thousand-mile separation (I live in Colorado, they in Boston), time together is limited and communication is difficult. The good news is that I truly believe my mother knows I love her and I have forgiven her. This was the thing I wanted more than anything in this life.

At times I still to struggle to maintain compassion for her, but at a deep level, when thoughts of her come into my mind, something inside me has changed for the better. I am now able to stop my mind from plunging into a pit of darkness and hostility.

Another by-product of getting free of my resentments of my mother has been the release of my own creative energy and voice. I am longer choking on my own bile.

My daughter and I just got back from a two-thousand-mile road trip to Los Angeles to help my mother's only surviving brother bury his lover of fifty years. While we were with him, he showed us some pictures of our family of origin and told us some stories about my mother as a young girl. The picture that touched me most was a beautiful snapshot of her young teenage self, smiling through sad eyes, for she too had come from a violent alcoholic home. I felt an abiding tenderness for this young girl who never got to tell her own story. When we arrived home there was a message from my mother thanking us for helping her brother and telling us she loves us.

When I met Brad Blanton four years ago, I told him and the group that the only thing missing in my life was five minutes of honest conversation with my mother. After waiting for over fifty years for that conversation, he showed me how to initiate it myself, how to give up my victim identity for an identity as a powerful, loving, capable individual. I like myself this way. Thanks Brad. And thanks to the entire Radical Honesty community for helping me to reconnect with what is essential in myself.

Love,

Averill Bowers

What I am up to today: *I am a writer and a golfer and I travel across the country in a van named Charlie. At least once a year, one of my adult children will take the trip with me. While we are on the road, we have wonderful, and sometimes not so wonderful, experiences, and I write about them. Each year I report our most interesting adventures in a Christmas letter, sort of. Think of it as the Christmas letter from Hell.*

This year I am working on a play titled "Donnybrook Fair," about the insanity of unresolved intense sibling rivalry between sixty year olds. Another play is in the works concerning my completion with my mother. I just finished a piece called "Son of the Lone Ranger," which was written for radio.

The thing I like to do best is to share some of what I have learned in this strange experiment called life. I keep on track, willing to learn what I need to learn about myself and be productive giving everything I've got to help make this world a safe and loving place for all of us. To this purpose, my daughter and I are starting a Radical Honesty group here in our town. Our goal in this group is to search for deeper levels of compassionate interaction in everyday life and to have megatons of fun in the process.

14 CHRIS:
AIDS, Death & Dad

I n the summer of 1994, David and I went to Germany to attend the baptism of my niece. I asked him to travel with me because I wanted to get to know him and become his friend. David is my ex-husband Joerg's lover.

Joerg and I had been married for 15 years and had 4 beautiful children when I left him for a man I had fallen in love with. His initial understanding attitude was short-lived. He quickly started a gay relationship with David, and, for the next five years, we struggled with our deep-seated resentments for each other.

With Brad's help we finally told each other the truth, spoke our anger and fear and came to love each other again. We tried to get back together three times over the next two years. Each time, David had to move out of Joerg's house. Each time, Joerg got scared, manipulated and lied in order to keep his two lovers, and finally fell out of relationship with me. Right before the final time we tried to reconcile, we found out that both men were HIV-positive. We were devastated, cried a lot and still tried to get back together. After that, I quit for good.

I hated David. Not only had he given the father of my children and the man I'd shared my life with a deadly disease, but I also held him responsible for the destruction of the possibility to heal my family.

Several months after we found out about the HIV positive results, I called everyone together to participate in a three-hour family therapy session with Brad. There was Joerg, David, my two teenage daughters, my ten-year-old son, and myself. When we came into the office everyone was scared but nobody ran away. We all had a chance to tell each other the truth about our resentments and our disappointments. A lot of pain and hurt was finally directly addressed and everything was talked about. The children resented David for "killing" their dad, and their dad for being careless, and all of us for upsetting their lives over and over again. We all cried (including Brad) and were angry, and resented and appreciated each other. Then, three hours later, we went out to dinner.

Nevertheless, over time, I noticed that I was still holding on to my resentments for David with a passion. He made a fine scapegoat, which let me off the hook. I did not want to take on the responsibility for the relationships in my family. I liked it that the children felt uncomfortable with David, and, in subtle but distinct ways, I supported their judgmental attitude against him. That way, I did not have to deal with my hurt, my feelings of failure, my rejected femininity, the ending of a 20-year relationship and all the dreams associated with it. This was what was actually going on, and I knew that if I did not get over it, the children wouldn't either. The battle would continue and the unhappiness would persist. I had to forgive David in order to go on with my life and to allow for loving relationships between the children, their father and their father's partner.

My vision for my family was that everyone would accept and support everyone else, and David was a part of the family now.

That is why I asked him to go to Germany with me. We were both very scared. We had good times and bad times, and we are friends now. I do not love him as much as I love Joerg, but he is accepted into the family and the children are fine now. We celebrate birthdays together and some holidays. Sometimes we get upset with each other just like in every other family. I am committed to clean it up as we go.

Chris is a massage therapist, mediator and mother of five.

15 LEO:
Love in the Afternoon
...Any Afternoon

I am lying with my friend, Patricia. We just had sex. It was great sex, a little kinky, very passionate and fun, too. We have been coming to her apartment to make love or sleep for over a year now. Her apartment is a part of supportive housing at 8th Avenue and 43rd street in a neighborhood known as Hell's Kitchen in Manhattan, a long block or so from Times Square, and two blocks from the Theater district and Broadway.

Patricia and I met during the run of a Broadway play. She was an understudy and I was one of the main characters. I was married to "Beatrice" at the time and fooling around as much as I could, drinking a hell of a lot and smoking my share of weed. Just escaping.

One afternoon, after a long session of lovemaking, Patricia handed me a copy of *Radical Honesty*. She said, "I think you need to read this." I did, and my life has changed completely. I will never be the same. The idea that telling the truth shall make you free had wandered around in my soul for a long time before I read the book. I had wanted to come clean and I didn't know how. The universe seemed to open up and say, "Okay, buddy, put your actions where your dreams are."

I read the book, then I read another book and I pondered and I thought. Then I called 1-800-EL-TRUTH. A real friendly voice answered the phone. I have no idea who it was, but I knew that I was on the path when she gave me Brad's e-mail address. I wrote some goofy letters about the gurus of truth and Brad responded by writing that there was a weekend session in Boston on such and such a date and to get on over there. I wrote back that I didn't have the money. He countered with, "I don't give a rat's ass if you have to steal hubcaps, get your ass to Boston. You can stay with me." Now, who in his right mind could refuse such an eloquent and articulate offer?

I finished the weekend and a little later on I attended an eight-day Course in Honesty workshop on a beautiful ranch in Virginia. I decided to tell the truth about who I am to Beatrice, my children, and the world. I appeared on the 20/20 TV show about Radical Honesty to lock myself in to my commitment to telling the truth, and I came clean with my wife and with my children.

I talked with my wife about how we were hiding the truth from each other. We talked about other women that she knew about and some she didn't know about. We talked about forgiveness, and the forgiveness part did not come around for a long time. I imagine that Beatrice, now my ex-wife, will never be able to completely forgive me; however, lately we are on better terms than we have ever been. I like her a lot more and I imagine that she likes me a lot more. We communicate about the children and each others' families and we sanely discuss matters that have to do with money, school, medical care, and so on — all the life stuff, as best friends would.

With that, my life has changed forever. Since I decided to lance the boil of a festering and poisonous marriage, and to reveal to everyone the truth about myself and have long talks with those I have issues with, my life has opened up. To my great relief, there is no hope, only being.

When I showed the life story videotape to my daughter, she was twelve. She was eating a piece of pizza and when the tape was over she looked up and said, "Dad, you didn't talk enough about your motorcycle trip." I asked her what she thought about the women and the drugs and she said, "I already knew about that."

My son, who was fourteen at the time, had a different reaction. He was livid at Brad because, at the end of the tape, Brad commented by saying that he thought my life story was bullshit and that I was a coward. I explained to my son that most memory is made up. I said that my behavior, all the fighting and doing drugs and womanizing, was a coward's way of avoiding a serious situation.

My children and I, who are now eighteen and almost sixteen, have an open, honest, loving relationship. We discuss sex, drugs and other personal matters openly. Beatrice and I are on better terms than we have ever been. I cannot say that this has been an easy trip. It has taken me to places of great despair. On the other hand, it has taken me to places of great spirituality and joy as well. It has been almost three years since I took the workshop and, in truth, I am still finding out about the truth, and I am pursuing it as it pursues me every day.

I know that I create it all—you, myself, and all the stuff that goes with it. For me, the trick is in the choices, and creation comes with every little notion. Radical Honesty is nothing more than a means of helping me to lift the veil of my opinion and judgment...a tool to help me wake up from this dream. So that, at last, I can forgive myself, and consequently all others, and love completely.

Leo Burmester is an actor. He's been in lots of Broadway plays and lots of movies, including Les Miserables, The Abyss, The Last Temptation of Christ, *and* The Devil's Advocate.

16

SUSAN:
Shadow Dancing
In the Light

When I first met Robert (a.k.a. Blue), I was already committed to practicing Radical Honesty. I had read the book, been to a two-day workshop, and completed some of my unfinished business with my parents.

Blue got my attention immediately because of his paradoxical approach to courtship. On our first date (our third meeting, but our first time alone), he told me that he really liked me and wanted to be with me, but that he was probably not a suitable partner for me because he had a very rigidly scheduled life that did not leave room for "normal couple activities." He saw me as a sociable, extroverted type, and imagined I would be frustrated with his need for alone time and his eating and sleeping schedule.

The way he talked about himself and his willingness to listen so openly, expressing his doubts about my being his girlfriend, endeared him to me right away. I wasn't used to such self-deprecating disclosures on a first date. His way of expressing himself was so real, so completely uncensored. Our conversation moved me to tears and to laughter. I had never felt such a freedom to be all of myself—that is, to reveal the parts of myself that I thought might scare him off: my fear of commitment, my unwillingness to commit to a relationship until we had experienced each others' shadow sides. As you might guess, I was carrying some baggage from past relationships where I had jumped in immediately with both feet, and later realized I hadn't been true to myself.

He took all this in stride—including the fact that I was going to continue to date other men until I had enough actual experience with each of them to make an informed choice. He hated it, but he was willing to endure the insecurities that this brought up. And I, because of my renewed commitment to radical honesty, was willing to risk losing this really cool guy and remain 100% true to my own timing and pacing with regard to commitment.

As our relationship progressed, I came to understand what he meant when he had said "my schedule probably won't work for you." It didn't. My daily routine is similar to most peoples'. His was quite different. The thing that didn't work in all this was finding a mutually compatible time to make love. In spite of this problem, I found him so far superior in every other way, compared to the other men I knew, that I let go of my other dating relationships, and focused exclusively on him as my guy. We managed to find enough times to make love, either by my staying up too late for what worked for me or by him messing up his schedule and doing it when I wanted it. The situation was frustrating for both of us, but there was a wonderful tantric energy that we shared during our evenings together, even when we did not have the energy or motivation to make love. We shared much physical and sensual pleasure—massage, cuddling, dancing, my doing yoga while he did chi gung. That seemed just as important as sex.

Because of my commitment to radical honesty, and because we both had a background in Gestalt Therapy with its emphasis on regular sharing of resentments and appreciations, the Romance Stage of our relationship looked, on the surface, to be less focused on harmony and more on realism. We began sharing resentments and appreciations early on as a way of keeping communication channels open and free of static:

"I resent you for being unavailable when I want to make love; I resent you for saying you can't make love until three hours after your dinner; I resent you for being so rigid! Whoops, that's an interpretation! I resent you for telling me I should sleep in the afternoon like you do, so I can make love at 2 in the morning."

"I resent you for not taking naps. I resent you for getting tired at 11 p.m. I resent you for falling asleep while we're making love! I resent you for not caring enough about my needs! Whoops, that's an interpretation! Well, I resent you for saying you won't make love after midnight."

After about a year, we were feeling less excited by our ability to be radically honest about our differences. His sleep disorder (my name for his shadow) and my selfishness (his name for my shadow) weren't quite as lovable as they had been during the Romance Stage. It became more difficult to keep regular with our resentments because now they were beginning to feel like a serious threat to the relationship.

Even though I knew that expressing resentments is not about getting the other person to change (it's about being fully self-expressed), still I secretly hoped that by hearing my feelings, he'd "see the light" and decide to change.

So we stopped sharing resentments daily and began doing it more sporadically. And then only occasionally. And after about another year, we broke up. In retrospect, I believe that if we'd stayed regular with resentments and appreciations; if we hadn't given up this practice because "nothing was changing," we never would have broken up. Because, when we were doing the practice regularly, there was realness in our relating. Sure, we were both frustrated and helpless, but we were being present with one another.

We were apart for a total of three months. Then, the movie "As Good as It Gets" came out. The character played by Jack Nicholson was in many ways similar to how I saw Blue (and how he saw himself). And I began to fall in love all over again with how open he was about his human foibles.

Anyway, soon afterward we reconciled, rationalizing our decision with the phrase, "Maybe this is as good as it gets." And we began to play those same broken records of resentment all over again. I was determined to continue sharing my resentments and appreciations on a daily basis in spite of the sinking feeling in the pit of my stomach, the hopelessness, that I got into every time I heard myself saying the same resentment in the same old way.

We told each other how much we hated feeling so deeply bonded to each other while at the same time feeling so depressed and hopeless—so powerless to change the other and so unable to modify what seemed to be our natural biological rhythms. As we explored these feelings, we discovered that we had been avoiding feeling the impasse we were in. We had been unwilling to "just stay with the helplessness." Honest self-expression had become just too painful. We had succumbed to the "broken record syndrome."

The conclusion we came to was that it is important to do our resentments and appreciations as a practice, not a strategy—as a daily discipline, an inner reality check, not as a way to get something "out there" to change.

This was about a year and a half ago. Here comes the happy ending. We actually succeeded in doing the "I resent/I appreciate" practice every day for about six months without any visible behavior change on either of our parts. It was difficult to keep up the practice—it seemed at times to be hurting us more than it was helping us, but we did it.

Then, one day, without any forewarning, Blue told me he had decided to make a major change in his eating and sleeping schedule—for health reasons. This change meant he would now be available to make love with me during the early part of the evening. The change on his part appeared to have no relationship to the fact that this was what I had wanted all along. I trust what he says—that it really was for health reasons. Still, I can see that sharing the resentments and appreciations every day as a practice created a profound shift in our communication. We had to let go of all hope of ever having control or "getting what we want." When our commitment was to simple and honest self-expression, rather than control, the power struggle just dissolved.

Thanks to Radical Honesty, I now feel the profound freedom that comes with letting go of control. How can I describe this freedom? Well, it's like relaxing instead of tensing up when I think I'm not going to get what I want. It's like relaxing into whatever degree of pain I feel, instead of exaggerating the pain or going into the familiar "I'm never going to get what I want" tape. And it's like being able to say "I resent you..." when Blue doesn't do what I want, without having to do anything about the resentment. And it's like loving Blue for being himself, and trusting that if I stay present, whatever I need usually comes to me—even if it's not always what I want.

Susan Campbell, Ph.D. is a psychologist and the author of six books, the most recent of which is Getting Real.

17

NOAH:
A Prose Poem

From an e-mail conversation on a Radical Honesty listserve:

Hello Roz, Noah here.

What are relationships for? For the last year or so my relationships are for teaching me how to put joy in my life. What they were before that, I don't know.

Already knew I was a liar when I came across Radical Honesty, just didn't realize how much of one. I did an 8-day over a year ago in California. Within 3 months of the workshop I lost more than half of my friends. I alienated my family, had a nuclear blow out, with my parents and my whole life turned upside down. I was shaken hard enough that several tons of horseshit, including most of my possessions, my dignity and my story of right and wrong, all fell loose. There's a lot more to come no doubt. Peter, this is for you too. There was nothing civil, pretty, polite or sweet about it. The sweetness came later. At the time, I had to be ugly or die. This is me right now. When I am quiet and polite, you can bet I'm lying! I still get ugly sometimes; only now I'm not as afraid of myself because I know that what is beautiful about Noah is in there too. Do I make the slightest bit of sense?

I made the same thing happen at work. I became jobless and even homeless for a while. I was living in total adrenal terror. Pardon the syrup, but those were the first best days of my life. With the help of a friend who practices Network chiropractic, I began to notice feelings in my body. Never did that before. So now, when I pay attention to how I feel, my relationships are each a kind of mirror. The great ones reflect my bullshit back to me so I get to see it. Telling the truth is difficult and scary. Sometimes it's like dying when I speak of how I feel. And then bliss pours into me like a deep, wet kiss.

Losing fear of revealing my resentments and judgments is how I am welcoming love into my life. Takes relationships to do that.

Peace, Noah

Noah works with the handcapped teaching them to ride horses. He is an activist against American policy in Iraq. His life is about compassion.

PART THREE

SETTLING THINGS
AT THE FINANCIAL SOURCE

Telling the Truth at Work
—Bosses, Employees, Peers

A Reformulation of Work Based on How You Want To Be at Work: A Change in Perspective That Comes from Honesty

This section begins with a story told by Paul LaFontaine, whose completion story with his parents was in Part One of this book. This story is an example of how, by transcending his previous limiting beliefs about who he was, and reformulating what he was doing at work, Paul changed his life at work. Paul took ownership of his job according to his vision of what he was about, which was made possible by discovering, through telling the truth, that who he is doesn't have to be dictated by the past, but can, instead, be designed according to a vision of the future.

Paul's project proves that the future is not destined to be a replication of the past, and actually makes us excited about the possibilities of our own lives. His reformulation of what he was about at work, through writing up his projects according to his vision, changed a disgruntled employee (with a recent moderately poor performance review) to a recognized significant player in the design for the future growth of his company. He also got a $2,000 raise.

Through being radically honest, people give up attempting to control their lives through controlling other people's impression of them, and thus give up, as well, the attempted manipulations that such an illusion of control requires. Because of that, when they identify themselves as the beings they are, rather than through their performance, from an onlookers standpoint, they become more capable of designing their own future. This turns out to give people actually much more control than they ever imagined in the old days. And by then, it doesn't matter as much to them whether they are in control or not. There is a progression in people's ability to be creative in designing their own future due to the freedom that comes from practice in being radically honest.

In the next story Paige gets fired. Paige and Paul both start telling the truth about what they think, what they feel and what they want to create. Paul gets promoted. Paige gets fired. Good for both of them! Much more important than job security is something called taking responsibility for creating your own future — win, lose or draw.

But even more amazing are the very short stories in this section, of incidents in which clearing and forgiveness occur and people just move on. It's as though a miracle happens and is hardly even acknowledged. These small instances are more precious, in a way, than the big decisive and notable life changing events. People learn the individual skills of honesty and intimacy, and it goes where they go and happens where they happen to be. If there is any such thing as applied enlightenment, here it is.

18

PAUL:
How Work Becomes Play

The chair was uncomfortable as I sat down. My boss had called me into his office for my annual performance review. Originally the company had hired me a year before to examine process efficiency in the facility. Instead, they wanted me to sit and write memos. Whenever a piece of furniture was purchased or moved, I had to do the paperwork, after which they bitched at me for not completing the forms to their satisfaction. It was boring work and it had me trapped because I needed the paycheck.

"Really, I wrote a better review," my boss said. "They changed it. There's nothing I can do."

"They're always doing things like this," I replied. "Can I write a rebuttal?"

"Yeah, but be careful," he said, handing me the review.

They deserved a rebuttal. They wrote that I had failed to document purchases satisfactorily. Of the many purchases I had made that year, only once had they caught me short of paperwork. My

This story is reprinted from the book *Practicing Radical Honesty*.

rebuttal would hammer this point and embarrass them with their lack of information. From my small chair in a cubicle amidst a sea of cubicles, a clever rebuttal took shape. Once it was completed and in the mail I prepared for a vacation.

My vacation was the Radical Honesty Eight Day Workshop. Brad Blanton spoke about stories, language, and personal power. He spoke of a life of play. He showed us how to meditate. He showed us movies. He talked about how we are the creators of our own experience. He put me in a chair and listened to me talk, coaching me to notice what I was experiencing. After several days, I noticed that in my mind I was blaming other people, "them," for my dissatisfactions. I learned. I learned about fear, responsibility, and telling the truth. I learned how to notice what came up for me emotionally. Most importantly, I learned about myself. As the workshop neared completion, I listened to Brad describe a technique useful in being a powerful creator. I heard him describe the writing of projects.

I was excited by his description. I organized furniture orders for the company into projects; but a project of my own was different. I could create my own life in my projects. After some instruction, I wrote my projects. In one, I recreated my work by writing a clear vision and measures of success with timelines. I would transform my work into play. I was going to expand on my furniture pur-chasing and become a creator of work environments that would transform the company from a sea of cubicles to an open space where teams would flourish. I called this project "Work Environment Creator." I would be unstoppable.

Project in hand, I returned to the company and began talking about work environments. I got out of my small chair, left my cubi-cle, and began walking around the building asking people what they needed to improve their workspace. I drew diagrams and talked about creating an open space where teams would flourish. I was excited by my vision and couldn't stop talking about it.

Prior to leaving for the workshop, I had been given a task to "coordinate and document company departmental involvement" on a $5 million office refurbishment. I didn't know what this meant, so I checked my Work Environment Creator project and decided that I had a better plan. I took charge.

I gathered the architect, consultants, and contractors together around a table and looked at each of them as I leaned forward in a large, comfortable chair. After a moment of complete silence, I spoke.

"This project is the first step in recreating this building as an open environment that supports teams," I said. "We will complete it and have our people move in on July 8th."

"OK," said the architect.

"Let's get to work," said a consultant.

I then said this to the management of the company and the people who would move into the space. I said it to my friends, strangers, and anyone who would listen. When quick decisions were needed, I was consulted and I said it again. When people rolled their eyes in meetings and expressed doubts as to whether a project this size could be finished on time, I said it yet again. I said it in the cafeteria. I said it in the restroom. I said it in my sleep.

On July 8th, our people moved in.

I listened as people told me what a good job I had done. I reviewed my project and was ready for more. I had a vision of the entire building being an open space that supported teams, so I set to work. Using learning from another project I had created and my experience at the Radical Honesty Workshop, I created a workshop where departmental managers for the company could develop a team-based work environment for their people. I visited the vice president of the facility.

"I am going to work with each department and develop a plan for creating an open, team-based work environment," I said. "I'll have these plans ready for future growth."

"OK," he replied.

I started giving the workshop. I was excited as I told the department managers about the advantages of an open environment. I had fun. I drew pictures for them from which they began modifying their workspace on their own. I applauded them. I talked about a team-based facility. I drew more pictures. I was slowly and steadily bringing my vision into being.

The executives decided they were going to build a new office building. I was assigned the project. I reviewed my project and prepared to create a work environment for the executive group. I met with them and talked about an open space in which teams could flourish. I talked about how I was creating this in each department. The group (the "they" of months before) sat and nodded their heads. "You are the example for the rest of the facility."

I concluded, "Your new space will be a team-based space."

"OK," said a vice president.

"Good idea," said a director.

"Can't disagree with that," said another vice president.

I was making my project with its vision a reality. I was creating work environments. I was having fun. I walked past an abandoned rows of cubicles that I was having disassembled and went on to my new office. I was comfortable as I sat in my large chair. I felt free. I smiled as I spoke to myself. I was playing.

Editor's Postscript: *One of the signs of transformation is that what once was Hell becomes fun. Paul transformed his relationship to work at his company by making a paradigm shift, a change in perspective that allowed him to recreate everything at work from that different perspective. He did what Robert Fritz, the brilliant author of four books* The Path of Least Resistance, Creating, Corporate Tides, *and* Life as Art, *calls a shift from the reacting orientation to the creating orientation. As a result of doing the workshop, Paul began the transformation from reacting to circumstances imposed upon him by his job, to creating his life at work.*

19

PAIGE:
Sometimes the Magic Works and Sometimes It Doesn't

I decided to make some noise at work. I decided to challenge what I thought needed challenging, which would either help create positive change or get my golden ass fired. I also decided that if I was going to get fired, I was going to get a pretty severance package while I was at it. So...I started talking, to anyone who would listen, about what was going on. That included my Plant Manager's boss, my bosses and my bosses' boss. I also told my Plant Manager, Jim, what I was doing and advised him that much of what I was talking about was my judgment about his inability to manage and lead the plant.

During these conversations I expressed a few appreciations, some empathy and a lot of resentments. One of my major resentments was based on my interpretation that each of them knew the plant was in deep do-do, knew that Jim was incapable of managing the plant and leading the effort necessary to turn things around, and knew that he was a divisive, lying sack of shit who'd done everything he could to destroy anyone who crossed him, and yet they were unwilling to do anything about him.

My co-workers were also talking with their bosses, some of who were the same people I was talking to. The only difference was that they weren't telling Jim about it. Needless to say, Jim was convinced that if he could just get rid of me, the only one he imagined didn't support him, he'd be A-OK. After six or seven weeks of talking with all these people, the Cavalry, a selection of high level HR and Operations Managers and Vice-Presidents, told us they'd decided that a visit to Jackson was in order. Duh! With an eye roll!

I was very much looking forward to what promised to be a freaking free-for-all of appreciations and mostly resentments culminating in a plan of attack with responsibilities and commitments by management and support teams. However, a week before the pow-wow, when Jim found out about the meeting, he panicked and quickly (and characteristically,) held individual meetings with his managers. They, the same people who'd been talking to their bosses and asking for help, quickly and characteristically dummied up, chickened out and pretended they knew nothing about it. When he came to my office to tell me about the meeting I told him I already knew about it.

He used his normal intimidation tactics which usually included scenarios such as I would lose my job because I was unaware that the Cavalry couldn't be trusted. He said he was the only one I could trust as he was always trying hard to protect me and had, he claimed, in fact already saved my job once... blah, blah, blah. This time, I didn't listen to the shit and for 40 minutes expressed as many resentments as I could in between his interruptions, excuses, threats, lies, and basic bullshit. Halfway through the meeting he started backing out of my office. After about 40 minutes, he literally ran from my office. No kidding, I'm in the middle of expressing a resentment and he opens the door and dashes out. I yelled after him that I resented him for bagging out on the conversation.

I won't bore you with the petty details of the 40-minute shouting match. I will tell you that I felt myself again for the first time in several months. I felt powerful and in control. And Jim was scared shitless. I have to admit that his fear felt good.

That was on a Friday. I had a great weekend even though I knew Jim spent the entire weekend soliciting support. God love him, he even asked a few hourly employees he knew didn't like me if they'd be willing to tell Paige stories to the Cavalry!

On Monday, I started packing my personal stuff, cleaning out my computer and organizing my files. I got the call from my HR bosses that afternoon. They were coming in the following day to discuss my conversation with Jim. (These are the same people who earlier offered me an opportunity to leave when I challenged the decision to give me a 5% increase on a "highly effective" review against higher increases for my male counterparts with just "effective" reviews.)

When they got there, I told them that over the last year Jim and I had had the same conversation—politely and in small bits—only the most recent interaction had included all the pieces, and was loud. I told them the difference was that now he knew he had to answer to his bosses about results and didn't want me at the meeting giving my take on the situation, or encouraging others to do the same. To my credit, I didn't pretend I wasn't part of the reason the plant was failing and that the lack of partnership between Jim and I was a crucial stumbling block. Even though all those people had been talking about our facilites' problems, and Jim's obvious inability to deal with them, my bosses made it clear the company was not ready to move on Jim. So, I offered to leave amicably for a substantial but fair severance package.

Then the cheap, stupid, sons-of bitches low-balled me! Can you fucking believe it? So I told them I wasn't leaving for that and we'd have to figure out another way to solve Jackson's problems. Then they really hurt my feelings, pissed me off and further damaged their future defense against my court case by telling me if I didn't quit and take the package, they'd fire me and I'd get nothing! What idiots. I offered them some other alternatives to protect my own legal position and then told them I'd negotiate with their boss since they'd offered what he'd authorized them to offer. The dickheads forget that they shouldn't fuck with the HR Manager. I mean geez guys, I know all the secrets. They say they're going by policy and I can quote the seven times they've gone outside of it in the last six months...And produce documents with their signatures on them! So, long, stressful story short, I packed my boxes and left. (To add insult to injury, they wanted me out that day! The bastards!) Ten days later I had a signed severance package for a week's more severance than I'd originally asked for and a Christmas bonus.

I've been officially unemployed since December first. And, as an added bonus, in the state where I live, I can collect unemployment while I'm on severance! Can you stand it? I'm making a thousand more a month for not working than I was when working. On May 1, I'll get my last paycheck. In the meantime, they're still insuring me and contributing to my 401K. So I'm on a five month paid vacation.

I have heard from four recruiters today. I'm being clear about my needs but know that I'll have to keep fighting myself to ensure I don't try to please others by convincing myself an opportunity may work when my gut tells me it won't. In other words, exercising that magic word, NO!

I'm taking care of myself, exercising regularly, eating fairly well. Andy has been abundantly supportive, and we're both looking forward to what we'll create next.

Editors Note: *Paige didn't quite make it to forgiveness yet. She got a good result, but still has unfinished business with her former boss and still relishes the rightness of her position a little too much. I like her story very much because it reveals some of the complexity of working through to forgiveness. It also shows how direct and honest expression of judgments, along with feelings related to the judgments, doesn't always* *work out to be a bed of roses. However, you can still get some practical results that are ahead of the less practical; but ultimately the big goal is the important matter of forgiveness. Until that process completes itself it is likely that Paige will be in for a little more conflict with future bosses than needed; but I have faith that she will take care of herself fine in the process and will move another step forward the next time through.*

20 CHRISTINA:
Chrissie Becomes
Christina at Work

Well, I have a good one for you today. On Monday morning when I came into my office on the later side of 9 A.M., my boss said to me, "You deserve a spanking." And we laughed and he gave me a hug and then put both his hands on my ass! He has never done anything like that before and I was taken aback. I told him, "That isn't a very nice thing to do!" and he stepped back. Though I imagine he realized that he had crossed a line, and he quickly laughed it off and went to his office.

Nothing more was said about "the incident" that day, but I noticed that I was short with him about some detail he pointed out on a quote I sent too. I was still annoyed with him the next day and I imagined he was annoyed at me too. In the back of my mind I was quietly turning everything over in the meaning making machine, but didn't say anything, or even admit that "the incident" was bothering me. I told Katherine (my friend from the workshop) about the ass-grabbing Monday night and we puzzled over his behavior, but even then I didn't acknowledge how much it bothered me.

Yesterday, I had a question about something I was unfamiliar with, he said, "I can't believe you asked that question, you know better," Well, I was defensive and I asked him if he was aggravated with me about something else and he said 'no' and wanted to know what had been up with me lately. I took a deep breath and told him, "I wasn't going to say anything but I realized that when you grabbed my ass the other day, that really bothered me." Then he said, "I'm sorry and I shouldn't have done that." I sat there looking at him and tears started rolling down my face. I just sat there keeping eye contact and said, "I don't know what to say." He responded with, "Well, let's get some work done," so I got up and went to my office and sat at my computer while the tears just streamed down my cheeks. I felt like shit, I felt scared and mad, and then I noticed I was "shoulding" on myself.

Several times that day, Charlie (my boss) he asked me if I was okay. I wasn't and said I felt weird and speechless. Before I left for the day, he said, "Are you sure you don't want to say anything to me?" When I said I didn't he responded with, "Well, I thought you were the radical honesty girl." I said, "Well I guess I'm not that good at it," and I left.

Lucky for me I was meeting with my counselor whom I hadn't seen in a couple months, so I felt better telling her about what had happened. I felt clearer and no longer wanted to judge myself; I knew that I would come in today and, if I felt ready, I would clear with him using the resent/appreciate method. He actually opened the conversation with, "Well, do you have any residual feelings to deal with?" And I just jumped into it with "Yeah! I resent you for grabbing my ass the other day! And I resent you for saying 'I was just kidding around'! And I resent you for saying, 'I thought you were the radical honesty girl!'"

I felt my stomach tighten and my shoulder muscles contract; my foot tapped a couple times on the floor and I noticed my left hand lightly tapping my left leg—for emphasis, I imagine. I reported some of these body sensations and Charlie then asked me, "Why do you think you feel that way?" I told him I resented him for asking me why I felt that way and I felt my jaw tighten and I felt angry and I told him. He launched into a monologue about communication and why it was important to understand what I was feeling and get over it. Blah blah blah. I let him talk and then I said something defensive and something sarcastic. He let out a disgusted snort and turned to leave the room. I acknowledged my poisonous comment and told him that to get over my feelings, I wanted to concentrate on feeling them fully and express them to him until I didn't feel them anymore. Then he came back, stood about 4 or 5 feet in front of me, looked me in the eye and said nothing while I resented him several times for the three things I mentioned above. I kept eye contact and reported my body sensations and kept at it. I appreciated him for standing there silently and for the way he was looking at me, so I continued.

I paused for a couple minutes and reported noticing that I wanted to hug him and that I felt weird about wanting to do that. Then I felt tears coming in my eyes and I told him I felt sad and afraid that there would be weirdness between us. I felt my lower lip tremble and tears ran down my face and we continued to look at each other. I began to feel a sense of tension draining away down my legs. I reported the feeling of my stomach loosening, and I looked for whether there was tension lingering and reported some in my jaw.

We continued looking and I began to feel a sense of seeing him clearly as a human being, a being just like me. I began to smile and I felt my eyebrows go up a little. I reported more relaxing body sensations and we just looked at each other. I felt a giggle bubble up, I let it out and told him I imagined I looked silly standing there grinning. He said nothing and I continued to feel the effects of clearing and feeling happy. I told him I imagined he had something to say and he said, "Yes, but no." I resented him for saying "Yes, but no" he looked down, thought for awhile and said finally, "I think I probably care about you more than most people in your life, but you keep me at a distance." I said, "I know how much you care about me and I care about you differently than you do me." With that we got back to where we have stood from the very beginning.

I imagine he would like it if things were different and if I wanted to be with him as more than a friend. AND (this is a big AND) I did not feel obligated to respond to him in any way other than what was true for me. I could let him be just as he is. AND I could honor myself and let myself be just as I am without apology or judgment. What a concept! I think that may be what we are doing.

Love, Christina

Christina is the mother of two girls, pretty much the one who runs the show at work, and now in an intimate and powerful personal relationship.

21

KAY:
Ain't Nobody's Business But My Own

The most outrageous thing occurred the other day. Being a massage therapist and self-employed in a city that's swamped with very competitive massage therapists, I was making some calls to clients I hadn't seen in awhile to drum up business so I could pay my bills. I called this particular male client, told him I had missed him, wondered if he was OK and asked how he was doing, and when he was coming back for a massage. He started telling me that he had been really busy with work, watching his money situation, etc. At every turn I found a reason to give him as to why he needed to make another appointment. Finally, after a few minutes on the phone with him he said, "OK, go ahead and set me up with an appointment."

When I hung up from talking with him, I sat back feeling somewhat relieved that I could at least rely on his appointment to help me pay a bill, and then it hit me just how much I had manipulated this man. It was hard for me to admit that not only to myself, but then I knew I needed to admit it to him. (I remembered Brad saying during the 8-day that admitting when we're manipulating someone is being "radically honest.") Knowing I couldn't even think twice about it, I just picked up the phone, called him right back, and told him that I had to be honest with him. I told him I realized I had been very manipulative him during our conversation. I also said the truth was I had bills to be paid, that work had been slow, that I needed his money and all the nice words I'd said to him were an attempt to get him to make an appointment. I then told him he didn't need to come in, and that I totally understood if he wanted to cancel. He said, "No, Kay...I still want to come in and I really didn't feel manipulated. I'll be there for my appointment." When he came in I explained to him how difficult it was for me to call him back and to admit that I had been manipulative, and that it was new for me to be that honest with someone. We had a long and great discussion about what it means to be honest. By being honest with this client, a space opened up for us to be more real with one another. Thanks, Brad, for showing me it's okay to be uncomfortable and just do it anyway.

Kay Strayer is a massage therapist, breath worker and radically honest businessperson in Charlotte, North Carolina.

22 RAVEN:
Completion With a Former Lover At Work

O kay...I promised I'd share what happened when I went to Chicago to do a completion. I've been too "busy," intentionally, in order to avoid sitting down to report this to you all, living in the story that I did not want to have these strong emotions here at work; now I'm giving that up.

When I went to Chicago (for the convention) I was terrified because half the people who would recognize me knew me when I was 100 pounds lighter. The guy I went there to complete with was someone I once worked for, and whom I'd lived with for 6 months. I imagined he would see my being overweight as a sign that he made the right choice to tell me he could never be with me. Well, first of all, I did get jolted when several people flat out didn't recognize me. However, discovered that I felt OK if I made it a game. I'd go up to them and say, "So what have you been doing in the past 8 years while I've been getting fat?" That took the edge off for me and up front we acknowledged what we might have wanted to avoid.

I discovered how truly loved, valued and appreciated I was. I mean that huge company (there were 900 people there) was using three programs I'd created in just one city, and using them on an international level. I discovered my name was "legend." I was also asked to "give a three minute motivational talk." So I introduced the room to Radical Honesty, invited them to check out the web site, requested that the managers take a workshop, and that they make Radical Honesty workshops available for their sales people. (I also got hired to do some training for the office where I used to be sales manager in Colorado. I'll be going there in December with a case of *Practicing Radical Honesty* books!)

Okay, getting back to my completion conversation. I'm still unsettled by what I discovered, especially since I hadn't spoken to this guy for 8 years. On the second day of the convention I came out of the morning session and he was standing by the stairs. I had to pass him to get to my next program, and I knew this was the best moment to act. He was alone, his young wife was nowhere in sight. As I walked up to him, I saw a look flash through his eyes and I immediately imagined he thought, "How fat she got!" and, " I'm glad I didn't keep her in my life." So I asked him, "How are you, really?" the same question I used to ask him that meant it was time to have an honest conversation. He smiled and said, "I miss you. I've looked up your web site and I'm impressed." I noticed his face was red, his breathing shallow, his hands were trembling and he was tapping his left foot repeatedly. I noticed my mouth was dry, I had a lump in my stomach and I felt hot all over, like ants crawling on my body.

I said, " Bullshit."

There was a pause. We held eye contact. I took a breath.

He said "My father died" and tears welled up, then he added, "I did get to see him right before he died and I feel good about that." I said, " I appreciate you for sharing that with me, and I appreciate you for the way you look."

He said, "I'm trying to start a family."

I felt a flash of heat like lightening rush from my head through my entire body and suddenly I was so angry I was shaking. I really wanted to hit him. (The story in my mind is that after living with me, when he confessed I was the only woman he'd ever loved and the only one he'd ever been honest with, he then told me his parents would never approve of me because I was three years older, divorced, no family wealth and I already had 2 kids. He then started dating a girl 13 years younger from a wealthy family, told me he was going to marry her but that "nothing had to change" between us—we could continue to be lovers if she never found out. I said NO, and, many, many other choice words. He also told people we were never lovers.)

I said, "I resent you for ...(all the things I just told you)...I resent you for telling your business partner that you were not in relationship with me, I resent you for saying you never had sex with me, I resent you for telling her (the wife, girlfriend at the time) that our relationship was 'all in my head' and that you never were involved with me in any way! You lying son-of-a-bitch. I resent you. I RESENT YOU! I RESENT YOU! You are an asshole! A big fucking asshole! And I resent you..."

My heart was beating. I was breathing hard. Then ... silence. I felt clear for a second like you do right after you vomit. Sort of empty. My hands unclenched. I tingled. I felt cleared of the anger, but then, immediately after that precious few seconds of Ahh, I felt worse, far worse, I felt heavy in the chest, hard to breathe, light-headed, heavy like the gravity increased and SOOOOOOOOOOOOOO SAAAAAAAAAD.

In that instant I GOT how when I'm furious, I sit in the rage to avoid feeling loss, feeling sad, feeling pain. I'd rather be angry! And now I hated it that the anger was gone. I "knew" that about myself, but I GOT it this time. Then I felt fear. Massive tingling. I said, "I'm sad to say that I miss your friendship. I appreciate you for all the times you sang for me. I appreciate you for the sex we had in the park, and in the office. I appreciate you for the way you touched me. And I miss you."

He said, "I AM an asshole. I miss you too, and I can't do anything about it. I'm not willing to rock the boat. I would like to be friends."

I said, "I would too and I don't want to create the possibility of a rerun. I'll sit with that idea, though. I feel afraid and I'm very very sad." He said, "I am too."

There was another silence, and I felt related, vulnerable and okay just being there looking at him. Then he changed the subject and we talked a bit about his family and the company. As we parted, we both had tears in our eyes and I said I'd call the office before the end of October.

I'm now uncovering lots of places where I have this horrible sadness sitting in my body. I'm being with it and I don't like it. Even writing this now my eyes are wet and I'm swallowing hard. I'm clear that I don't want to let myself get too close to people to avoid the suffering of having them die or leave. And God knows everyone will do one or the other. So, it's either be alone or get over it. I'm not over it completely yet. And I feel so alone much more of the time than I've ever admitted, until right now. I felt that way earlier today when I sent my completion story to John (a fellow participant in the Course in Honesty). Then I thought, "What the hell, you're already crying, it won't kill ya, just keep typing."

I have a choice now that I see what's going on. I'm choosing to be with and express the sadness more often. I'm not letting myself pull back from others, and, I'm afraid. I am noticing how vulnerable and powerful I feel at the same time, and how happy and frightened I feel when I admit how much I love people and stay in that experience of love. It's a place of paradox. And it's okay to be here. I want to stay here. I love you and I'm afraid. But I won't let that fear stop me anymore. The love is all that counts.

Raven is a Radical Honesty trainer

PART FOUR

SETTLING THINGS
AMONG THE SORCERERS
The New Family:
An Honest Community of Friends

"I have to cast my lot with those who age after age, perverse-ly with no extraordinary power, reconstitute the world."
— Adrienne Rich

A Community of Friends

N ow that we have read stories of getting back in touch with and connection with the family we came from, the family we made through marriage, and the family we are in at work, we move further out to our network of friends. Then, in the final section we go even further out into the family of humankind. Like the Chinese boxes that fit into each other, from the smallest to the largest, the story grows from that initial love in the first family of life to full-blown compassion for the whole world. This trail leads from learning from real experience somewhere and somehow in your life, that intimacy can be tolerated, can be contagious, and can become the principle of organization; it can eventually even supersede greed as the primary organizing principle of collective economic life.

As we move from source family to the human family, the stories become more abstract and give way to interpretation. Perhaps this is because we just can't quite be as related, or feel as related, to larger and larger groups of people without turning the experience of being related to abstract principles of relatedness. Once the mind gets hold of anything experiential it tends to turn it into concept instead of an experience, and then a should, and therein lies a multitude not only of sins, but of religions and holy wars. It is the difference between the Golden Rule when it is generated through the honest contact of looking directly into the eyes of someone else, seeing that they are exactly like you and acting on that connection — and the principle that *"You should treat your neighbor as you would like to be treated,"* which leads to things like the crusades or terrorism or the American war on the children of Iraq. The connection with the experience of relatedness in our families of direct contact is what actually allows us to remain compassionate for the people of the world, rather than operating based on a principle of compassion which can so easily become doctrinaire moralism.

So I invite you to stay with us as we venture into the more difficult realm of forgiveness and love through honesty, expanded to the larger collective of us all, based on our experience of discovering the more practical aspects of love.

What follows is mostly letters to and from friends, with stories about what happens through honesty between and among them. Jack Stork's story from the back ward of a mental hospital is a simple and beautiful affirmation of honest sharing. In all the stories that follow after, there is this new luminosity that shows up in people and the world for all the people who have dared to become radically honest.

This section ends with a letter from me to our community of friends. It is a reprint from our newsletter, *The Radical Honesty Rag*, a few years back, to the community that has grown up around radical honesty. I was relaying news of my activities and also news of others in our community which some of the rest of us may not have known about. In the middle of writing this I realized what a family we had all become for each other. I was writing to my adopted brothers and sisters, aunts and uncles, nephews, children, and mothers and fathers, catching them all up on the recent family gossip and saying what was going on with me. I love my family. I love the one I have at home and I love the one I have all over the country, and to some extent all over the world. Whether I was the genetic source or the adopter or the adopted, what makes it work, when it does work, is honesty.

With enough light the shadows disappear. This is where love happens. It happens in the world between people who pay attention to each other and tell each other the truth. The stories of this love happening are so inspiring because we recognize immediately what is going on and say to ourselves or each other "what a beautiful story this is..." knowing in an instant why it is beautiful — because we have lived it in some moments of our own.

23 JACK:
Blind Truth

This Indian had congenital blindness, inherited it. His grandfather had it. He was telling me one time about his grandfather. He didn't want people to know he was blind, and he didn't want people to help him. He would walk on the soft shoulder of the road and find his way home. One night he didn't come back. He said, "We went looking for him in the morning. The county was building a bridge, and took the bridge planks out. He just fell down on the rocks."

The Sioux talk with a guttural sound in their throat: we went lookin for im. Pretty soon we find im. He was cussin. He was laughing his head off over this tragic incident. Name was Maize Waters, Kale we called him. We were both in an alcoholic treatment program in a state hospital. We grew up about 10 miles apart, but I never knew him. We all had work to do, serve supper and stuff. I come back one night, guy's standing there, hands in an Eisenhower jacket, looking out—I thought, "Poor sonofabitch, hallucinating." Fierce, tough-looking sonofabitch. I thought he was just new and

couldn't remember where his building was. He had some periph-
eral vision; he was always looking out the side of his eyes pretending like he wasn't blind so people wouldn't feel sorry for him. We
became friends. Guy who ran the place was kind of aggressive, he
says, "WE GOTTA GUY HERE WHO'S GOING BLIND. HE
CAN'T READ THE BIBLE, NEEDS SOMEBODY TO READ IT TO
HIM." I saw Kale flinch. Nobody responded, I knew that was hard,
so I said, "I'll read it."

They had a big dorm with two-man rooms. One guy would
leave and you'd inherit the other spot if you were lucky. I'd been in
there with an undertaker who was too far-gone to salvage. After he
left, I took Kale in and pissed everybody off—"What'd you put that
fuckin' Indian in there for, asshole?" The first night I saw him
undress, he had prison tattoos all over his body, dripping blood. I
was too scared to sleep. I knew he was uncomfortable too. I was
reading to him out of that Bible, it seemed like a bunch of bullshit,
beliefs and rituals, a fucking way of life. Rather stay drunk. I'd be
reading, and say, "Kale, this is a bunch of shit, isn't it?" He'd say,
"Yeah." So I went and got some talking books, got him *Tortilla Flats*.
This kid—I don't know where he was educated, but he knew
absolutely nothing, never read a novel—I suppose it was that
Catholic school out at the mission. I turned it on and left the room,
but looked in the door so I could watch his response, see if it would
be valuable to him. He was laughing and crying, almost pissed his
pants. First time in his life he hooked up with a book. It was a high
point for both of us.

Some Indian guys came to get him, said they needed a pitcher
for a softball game. I thought they were making it up, and just
wanted to go on a drunk. Next day they brought him back, sober. I
said, "Well, did you win?" He said, "Yeah." I said, "What kind of
shit is this, you're telling me you pitched a softball tournament and
you're blind?" He said, "The catcher, he kept talking to me.
Sometimes I had trouble, had to find the mound by feel. If the 3rd
baseman don't tell me where it is I have trouble. Somebody up, in
the stands saw me, and said 'That's Kale, he can't pitch, he's blind.'

So I took a bandana out of my pocket and put it over my eyes; I figure if they know I'm blind they hit me easy, but if I'm blindfolded they too scared to hit me."

We stayed up all night talking and laughing. I thought, what the Hell's wrong with me? The IRS is after me, my family left me, I lost my business and I'm in a mental hospital, and I'm laughin' and having the best time of my life. So was he. I thought, it don't matter what my circumstances are, my happiness is all internal. I thought, well what the hell, the human race is all lined up with the best ones in front, the worst in the back, and I'm the last motherfucker in the line, spent my whole life trying to move up two steps so I wouldn't be so conspicuous. I just thought, what the hell, I'll just be last. And I died. I saw a light in the darkness, you're free. When I woke up the next morning the world was luminous, light was coming from everything. I thought, we could just stay here forever, and Kale was running around laughing and chattering, very un-Indian like.

Jack Stork wrote this a year or so later: *Hey, Brad. After trying for 35 years I finally located Kale recently. He is living in Sioux Falls, SD. The Sioux talk deep in the throat like Chief Dan George* (Little Big Man *or* Outlaw Josie Wales). *When he answered the phone I said, "Kayo?" "Ya." I identified myself and he said, "I remember you, I remember you!" You are welcome to do whatever you want to with the story. Even with all the terrible stuff that was happening to me at the time, so many good things came out of it.*

24 RAVEN:
The Postman

I had a most unusual and wonderful experience with my mailman. When I left for the 8-day I requested a hold on my mail until my return (checks and bills lost for months by becoming bookmarks and note paper have caused much irritation in the past). I was supposed to pick up the mail to start service again; however, I found a pile of mail in the house when I came in Sunday night. I discovered that while the first two days of mail were delivered by a substitute, the regular mailman had noticed that my daughter was home and made the judgment call to continue delivering mail. So I went to the post office Monday, still high on Radical community living, and asked why my hold order had not been honored. I was told to wait for a manager. Eventually, my mailman came out and began to 'splain and give excuses for his decision. I stopped him in mid-sentence by saying, "I resent you for making that decision, for giving my daughter my mail, for ignoring the hold order and for the tone of your voice as you told me you made the decision! And, I appreciate you for coming out here yourself and being accountable to me for your actions."

He said, " I couldn't understand why you wanted your mail held and I'm so used to talking to both your daughters that I just figured it was okay. In fact I saw your older daughter there too, visiting and I used to talk to her a lot before she moved." I said, "I resent you for saying you 'figured it was okay'. I resent you for saying you 'couldn't understand why;' I don't give a shit if you understand why or not, you're not the one having to find the goddamn mail once the kids lose it in the goddamn house while I'm gone for 9 days! And I appreciate you for talking to my daughters, for remembering my older daughter and for delivering the mail at very nearly the same time every day."

He said, "Oh, I have 500 customers, and I remember lots of things. The girls boyfriends that leave then show back up; kids that run away and end up at your house; and I remember your older daughter complaining about how much she hated school and couldn't wait to move out of the house oh, but she never said anything bad about you or anything." "Bullshit!" I said, "I know Panda complained about me to you because she told me how much she talked to you!! I resent you for saying, 'she never said anything bad about you' and I appreciate you for all the times you listened to her complain about me."

"Well" he said haltingly, "Be mad at me for a while longer, then wave to me when you see me again, okay?" I said, " I'm not mad any more. I appreciate you for coming out here, for remembering my girls and the other kids that have been in my house, and I imagine that you're a really wonderful dad."

He got misty. I got misty. We smiled at each other a long time. The entire time it took to have this exchange no one was waited on, no one moved behind the counter. When I turned to leave, I noticed that both customers who were waiting at the counter were misty, so I smiled at them too. And I thought...YES, Radical Honesty works pretty good, most of the time....

25 JANICE:
Dumping the Layers Of Despair

For twenty years I had an eating disorder: bulimia. Bulimia is characterized by bingeing on large quantities of food and then purging—either by vomiting or using laxatives, or both. In my case it was the former. The other common denominator for those of us caught in the insidious web of bulimia is hating ourselves for doing it—big time.

After several years of trying to talk myself out of it, I eventually realized that if I did not get help, my eating disorder would kill me. I had to reach out—I knew I could not do this on my own. Hell, I'd been beating myself up for years already for what I perceived as weakness for not just stopping by myself. I finally let it go. So many years, so many layers, so much anger, so much despair, so much shame, so many relapses. So much lying!!!

For 20 years I rode a roller coaster that operated 24/7 and was piloted by fear, shame, control, and self-hatred. It was a brutal, destructive and horrifying experience.

As I began the journey of healing the, "so many layers" meant coming to terms with many issues in my life. Breaking out of being a victim and taking action to create a new and different adult experience is not only our birthright, but more importantly, it's our responsibility. A scary prospect for me!

Therapists, healers, workshops, 12-step programs—I did it all. And learned so much and healed so much and I was still bulimic. Bulimia, for me, was the ultimate in lying and withholding. To consume that much food, to furtively buy it, to throw it up, to spend the time and energy to orchestrate all of this—and still "appear normal," well, that's quite a feat. And, in fact, I was perceived as being capable, competent and successful along the way! No one knew in my "real life"—I told no one the truth. I set myself up to hate myself even more by telling myself "if they only knew, they would see the real me, they would see what an impostor I am, how unworthy I am of their friendship, their respect, their love."

In the early '90s I went for three and a half years without purging—a period I now recognize as abstinence, as opposed to recovery. I began bingeing and throwing up again in late '94. I was devastated. I made an even bigger liar out of myself by pretending that I was still "recovered"—would even lie openly in situations where there was direct questioning or sharing. I just wanted to shrivel up and die for the shame of it all.

I still continued the healing work, and I still did not share the truth with anyone except one therapist/healer. My life was not working—I was in a lot of pain and feeling miserable. I wanted so much to share the truth, especially with one work colleague, who was also a very close friend. So many things prevented that, especially my ego, my fear. I did not want to be perceived in any way as less than how he saw me, or as flawed, as weak, as "sick." What if he loved me less?

With coaching, I began considering telling the truth to this person, as well as two other people in my life with whom I was very close. Finally, I just did it. I told all three of them. I let go of the fear of what they would think of me and stepped into the void. The day that I opened the floodgates is one of the greatest things I've ever done for myself. The pain, the shame, THE TRUTH – all came tumbling out. What a relief! I felt energized, free and scared. Yikes, now I would have to take responsibility for myself—something that I had not exercised before!

After 20 years of my eating disorder having power over me, I had begun to turn the tables. It no longer had control. By telling the truth to people I loved, while I was still actively bulimic, I began the reclaiming of my power. In terms of my eating disorder, no longer living the lie released the vise grip that bulimia had had on me.

Very shortly thereafter, I told the truth and took a stand with someone who for years I'd unwittingly allowed to have "power over" me. I took a stand for my value, in a way that I'd not done before. I freed myself. I stood in the face of her anger, and her perception being different than mine. And I knew that that was okay for me.

The same willingness to be who I am and no longer keep secret what I do or think or feel ended my 20-year bout with bulimia. I say this with awareness of, and respect for, the power my eating disorder had over me, over my life. I know profoundly the insidious and destructive nature of eating disorders—and I am free.

I feel in my body that it is gone; none of the old energy that I was intimate with for 20 long years remains. I have "earned the right" to be here—not only alive but vibrant, thriving, whole—feeling like my life is just beginning.

The truth telling continues. As I move further down the road of recovery, I see more and more how my choices and decisions were often made by my eating disorder, and my eating disorder was rooted in lying and withholding. Today, as I notice, as I bring awareness more and more into my life, I get to make different choices, from a stronger and healthier place. I get to know the truth of my experience and consequently, myself.

I am loving life and all that it is for me. I am loving my new-found freedom. And I am especially loving myself.

Janice Beaton is a successful businesswoman in Canada.

Editors note: *Janice's story is here because it was being honest in her community of friends that finally healed her of what twenty years of help from experts couldn't, as long as she kept her secret.*

26

BRAD:
A Letter to My Friends

I n early July I went out to Boulder to give a talk on Friday night and run a two-day course I'd been invited to conduct at Naropa Institute. I was there for a number of reasons: (1) to give the talk about Radical Honesty on Friday night that would have an impact on how people live together, treat each other, and give them a taste of the nectar; (2) to enroll people in the two-day course at Naropa Institute which was to follow the talk; and (3) to enroll more people in the Boulder Eight Day Course in Honesty Workshop. About 60 people came to the talk, 20 of whom did the two-day course, 3 more enrolled in the Eight Day Course in Honesty in Boulder, and two couples signed up for the Radical Honesty Couples workshop in October at Sparrowhawk (my farm in Virginia.)

That first wing of my trip was a strategic success. It kept the business of the workshops going, gave us some money to live on, had a positive effect on the spreadsheets we are using to raise the capital to build the business of Radical Honesty Enterprises, Inc.,

This chapter originally appeared in *The Radical Honesty Rag,* the e-zine of the Radical Honesty community.

expand our database, etc. Also, as a kind of strategic objective side benefit, Taber, Sylvia and I met with two different corporations in the Boulder area to talk about corporate trainings with them.

After that I went to Albuquerque for a couple of days and did two great radio show interviews that were keepers. I then did another talk on a Tuesday night to about 40 people, and continued on to Tucson to do a very successful and inspiring half-hour television show. The talk was fine, and consequently the Albuquerque Eight-Day workshop became more than filled to capacity. The TV and radio shows expanded the database and sold some books in bookstores. I also gave a brief two-hour corporate introduction to radical honesty at Jim Cebak's construction company and made plans to do a one-day training there in September; and I came home with money. I was happy to keep the old strategic success-for-the-business ball rolling and encourage more people down the crooked path of honesty. But what really warmed my heart and blew my mind was something else. What I am proudest of, and in love with, and happy to report about, is what happened around the periphery of those strategic success stories. It was the ease and laughter and honesty of the conversation Taber, Sylvia and I had with eight people at our business meeting at the Whole Foods Store in Boulder; the way Sylvia and Taber both talked to people standing around after my talk; the excellent job Taber did of mediating and resolving two conflicts between me and two people in Boulder; and the way they both helped in the two-day workshop at Naropa.

What makes me happiest, when I look back on it, was the honesty, openness and the quality of the conversation around the dining room table at Michael and Andrea's house (including Michael's fifteen-year-old son) at the end of a long day. The ease with which we spoke about what we resented and appreciated (what most people would consider shocking truth), and the opportunity for that kid, at fifteen, to hear honestly how life was for us when we were his age, and how it is for us now. In Albuquerque, I got blown away again when we met for dinner at Jim and Nancy's house the night before my talk, where we drank some beer, ate good food and shared a joint a new friend had given me in Boulder. The eight of us just shared about life, love and work so easily and so clearly and with such inspiring honesty. Together sitting on the porch, we watched a storm come through and then went outside to sit in the hot tub. We talked, and looked at the afterglow of the sunset and then the stars. There were easy silences, quiet talk and occasional bursts of laughter with no pretense and no bullshit and no hurry to get anywhere.

It was the power I felt from the nourishment of these people that made the private conversation I had with the TV host at lunch in Tucson after the show so effective. I just told him what we had been doing and talking about when we hung out together. He removed himself from journalistic distance and and enrolled on the spot for the Albuquerque Eight Day Workshop that was coming up—for his own personal benefit.

These communities of support for radical honesty we have been dreaming of—communities that support people to live out loud—actually exist in the real world. They are not only at Sparrowhawk Farm during workshops, or at other workshop locations, or just during some of our songfests and parties. They are in Boulder and Albuquerque, New York and Los Angeles and in ongoing practice groups and casual informal meetings among friends in many, many other places right now. They are here, now. And they are not just sourced by Radical Honesty workshops or my books. Rather, our workshops and my books are sourced by a much bigger wave of change, where there is a new valuing of frankness and a devaluing of pose and pretense in the world. We are a small contributing part of something much greater, whose time is coming at an ever-quickening pace, in spite of the apparent incredible ignorance in the political and economic domain.

These groups of friends who don't have to pretend all the time are gradually steering the world towards a new paradigm for how people live together. We are showing how it is done by doing it. This is what I live for, and this is what I am grateful for, and this is what counts about what we are doing together to change the world. It's also been there in the weddings we have all attended together this year and in the songs that Amy writes and in the music we make together. It's in the way we are learning to work together. There is the spirit of willingness to share our lives as they really are—without shame and without pretense.

But, more than anything, it's permission. It's permission to live out loud from inside ourselves. It's permission for the great variety that we can all celebrate, that comes from us all seeing and knowing we do not all have to be the same. It's permission from outside, from other selves, who have given themselves permission from inside, to say what is on their minds and in their hearts. It is permission to let down our guard, to be among friends, to acknowledge our common being, and to really share what our lives are about.

What we continue to teach each other is that it's okay to be unique, unusual, different, or the same, odd or even, depressed or happy, mad or sad or horny or tired or angry or however we are at any given time. We also have in common a mission to share with everyone we meet what we have given each other and ourselves— permission to do more than we ever thought was permissible. We are here to give the world's people permission to live out loud.

We are at large in the world. What we are doing around the dining table, in the kitchen, at the talks, in the workshops, in the hot tubs, at the corporate meetings, on TV shows, in the radio interviews, in the mediations, at the weddings and in the private conversations, is the real thing, is our ultimate mission—which is permission. So, as it turns out, our strategic objectives and our ultimate vision are in complete harmony. Sonofabitch! Who knew? Isn't that nice?

The ultimate aim of my life now, and the shared vision of all the practice groups, graduates of all the workshops, investors of time, energy and money in Radical Honesty Enterprises, Inc., all the donors to our non-profit corporation, The Center for Radical

Honesty, and all the volunteers who help us—gets clearer to all of us as the days go by. This "mission of permission" we have somehow given within ourselves and received from each other we want to give to everybody else, because we want to play with them too, and create a world of permission for everyone. We're building on the success we have already accomplished, and even though it is excessively presumptuous, we presume, like a flea, crawling up an elephant's ass with rape on his mind, that we can do this for the whole world.

I, for one, am greatly encouraged and itching to get on with it.

Thank you for all of your help, to me and to each other. We are a cult. And some day we will take over the world.

Brad Blanton is a garden variety neurotic, a happy man and the editor of this book.

27

RAVEN:
The Lady at the Laundry

Three weeks ago when I went to do my laundry, the Woman Whom Everybody Hates was working. Margaret was running the place with her usual attitude, complaining in her thick German accent about the "stupid" customers, the "brats" playing in the aisles, her "ungrateful" daughter and that morning's news. I was in a particularly pleasant state of mind and thought I'd just go over and occupy her so she could leave the others alone and complain to me. I'd never really talked directly to Margaret before even though I'd seen her here and there in the neighborhood for years. So I said, " I imagine you're pretty pissed off. What's going on, Margaret?" Her eyes lit up and she told me about her daughter, her tough childhood, her health problems, her failures with men, her political opinion and how she hated "stupid" people. During her sharing, every time somebody would have a question or request, I took care of it so she could continue talking.

Every now and then when I felt moved I piped in. I appreciated her for her story, imagined that she was courageous, shared my own failures at marriage and just before I got my laundry together and left, I said, "You know, I had judgments about you and thought you were pretty mean. I'm really glad we talked. I really like you, and I acknowledge you for getting through a lot of the shit you've had to deal with—including this job answering the same questions every damn day. I don't think I could do it." She smiled. It's the only time in all these years that I ever saw Margaret smile. When she smiled I felt a rush of energy in my chest and my heart felt warm and a great wave of tingling moved through my whole body. My skin prickled. I left feeling really in love with life and the miracle of being.

Last week I went to do laundry and the owner was there working. Somebody said, "Where's the old battle ax today? Out chewing on nails?"

"Oh, Margaret? She died suddenly in her sleep last week. She's gone."

I felt my guts drop like being on a roller coaster. I felt my heart pounding. My hands got cold. I cried. I'm crying now as I tell you this.

Joy and Sorrow. They're not separate. You just don't get to have one without the other tagging along. Not that I didn't "know" that already. I just didn't have it as an experience this clearly before. So I am reminded. Life is a paradox. This is what my days have been like. The more I live here in the moment, the more I laugh, the more I feel in love, the more I cry. Every day there are opportunities to love. I am noticing places where I've been afraid and I'm now stepping in. The good news is, the love is at least as deep and usually deeper than the sorrow. Knowing that however, doesn't take away the fear.

Raven

Chrissie's Response to Raven's Story

Dear Raven,

I appreciate your story about Margaret. I appreciate you for saying that you helped customers who came up with questions so she could keep on talking to you. Thank you for sharing this. It illustrates what I've been experiencing too. The more I open myself up to people, I feel so much more of everything. Some days I am feeling so connected to others and so blessed with acknowledging their being—that the happiness fills my heart to overflow. This is great and overwhelming for me as I've hidden out for so long. I have been noticing how easily moved I am to tears in this open state. I was on the treadmill running one morning with my Walkman on, and *Bare Naked Ladies* playing. I love their lyrics, their humor and authenticity. As I listened to the song, "What a Good Boy," I found myself all choked up with tears in my eyes. I feel so susceptible, exposed and full of feeling.

I appreciate you for saying, "The more I live here in the moment, the more I laugh, the more I feel in love, the more I cry." I can totally relate to that. I appreciate you for saying "The good news is, the love is at least as deep and usually deeper than the sorrow and knowing that doesn't take away the fear." I am afraid too and I needed to verbalize that and get it out in the open. I appreciate you for saying you were feeling sad and lonely and wanted to be held. Thank you. Thank you. Thank you. O O O X X X

Love, Chrissie

Brad's Response to Chrissie and Raven

Dear Chrissie and Raven,

We, who are emotionally labile about the magnificence of being, huddle together unable to contain the uncontainable immenseness of it all, like a microbe at the foot of Mount Everest, aware of it all, trying to remain small so we can survive, until one day some wind blows us away and we become finished with the task of being present and resisting being present.

Like finely tuned voltage regulators for God, thermostats for Christ, laundry ladies for Raven, Raven and *Bare Naked Ladies* for Chrissie, Raven and Chrissie for Brad, and Raven, Chrissie and Brad for everyone we know, we share our wonder, our fear and our knowing of each other for a while and then we are gone. Love and death come and go. And all there is, is flow and flow and flow and flow.

I always wonder what the world would suddenly be like if we were all present at the same time to each other's presence to being, to the temporariness of it all, to our own passing away, and to the passing away of all things. I yearn to see and believe that people whose compassion for being has been awakened can share it until all people have it, but death seems to stay one step ahead of us. I am not complaining. I love us. And I may yet come to love death as just as much as anything else that comes with being. When I let being be, it contrasts with how I just almost always try to make something of it. Like Chrissie and the Bare Naked Ladies, the tragedy of mind and its attachments and its affinity with death overwhelms me. I am reminded of a poem by Lawrence Ferlinghetti—

The world is a beautiful place
to be born into
If you don't mind some people dying all of the time
or maybe only starving to death some of the time
which isn't half so bad, so long as it isn't you.

Yes, the world is a beautiful place
to be born into
If you don't mind a few dead minds in the higher places
or a bomb or two, now and then, in your upturned faces
or such other improprieties as our name-brand societies
are heir to...
with their men of distinction
and their men of extinction
and their priests
and other patrolmen

and their various segregations
and congressional investigations

and other constipations
our fool flesh is prey to.

Yes, the world is the best place of all...
for making the fun scene
and making the love scene
and making the sad scene
and going swimming in rivers on picnics in the middle of the
summer...
and just generally living it up.

But then, right in the middle of it all, comes the smiling mortician.

PART FIVE

SOURCING A WAY TO SETTLE AND SOURCE THINGS AMONG THE SETTLEMENTS OF SORCERERS

Transformation of the Larger World Community

The Big Picture:
Social Transformation

Well, this is the end of the trail of stories. This section is a big shift for any reader, and if you want to just stop here please feel free to do so. We have come to the part about the political and economic ways we poor pathetic human beings have worked out about how to live together. It is not a pretty picture and the story of our possible or likely recovery from the big habitual story we call our culture is not a pleasant one to hear. It is hard work and it requires more than our usual ignorance to comprehend. If you do continue, it is only fair that I tell you in advance that I have seeded this introductory essay to the final section with memes, which will infect you, and which you will not be able to forget for a long time. We are talking about the biggest story of all, the story of humanity, but this whole section is not like reading the stories that led up to it.

It is possible, of course, for anyone to live in a little enclave of people and not have to deal much with the world outside of that enclave. Most middle class people in the West, among the two percent of the population that controls forty percent of the wealth, have been able to do so for some time. Compassion ruins that. It becomes increasingly difficult to do, once you have become compassionate, even though your compassion may have at first been only for those in your own enclave. Compassion seems to spread whether or not we wish to allow it to do so. Not that we need the trouble. It is a pain in the ass to care for all the suffering people of the world. It is miserable to have to put up with all the true believer assholes that make up the pathetic mass of humanity — particularly the rich ones who contribute so much to the maintenance of the suffering — and then to feel having pity for them adds insult to injury. But it is possible, and it starts with paying attention to yourself.

If you can get dumb enough to just pay attention to being alive in your body, related to gravity and other people, moment to moment — and do that, just for a while — you have a chance of being happy, productive and contributing to others and getting joy from it. Compassion comes from being present to experience and to each other. If we can do this, rather than simply livimg in our minds, which are often the very source of ignorance — we have a half-assed chance of helping ourselves, our friends and the whole world. But most of us, most of the time are too smart to get over our ignorance. A mind is a terrible thing. Waste it.

To even talk to you or anyone else about this seems futile. But we have to talk about it. I am the founder of the Futilitarian Church. I am the Pope (the Pope of no hope). (Every member of the Futilitarian Church is the founder and also the Pope.) So I take on this futile task with relish, and probably not for the last time, here at the end of this book.

Being dumb is the cure for ignorance. Noticing happens then. But most people think dropping beliefs and getting dumb is a bitter pill and avoid it at all costs, and preferring their habitual ignorance like an electric blanket, to shield them from the cold hard facts of life. But I and some of my dumb friends have been re-

formed. We have seen the light and vice versa (lighted the scene —
or the light has seen us).

I love being dumb. I hate ignorance. I hate ignorant people too,
but I can get over it, and I do, and I think it's the way to go. But you
have to be a dummy to do it. Here is how I do it. I get mad. And
then I get over it. Why? Because I'm a dummy.

Okay. Enough of that. Let's start from the very beginning again,
to see if we can find some wisdom about dumbness. The awareness
continuum can be divided into three parts: (1) what you notice in
the moment about sensations in your body; (2) what you notice in
the moment outside of your body in your immediate surrounding
environment; and (3) what you notice in the moment in your mind.
That's all. That's it. That's all there is to notice, period. Radical
Honesty is reporting what you notice. That's all. Simple. Hard to
do. Why? Because we are too smart. We've been trained. We think
we know what we're doing. We have all kinds of bullshit beliefs in
our own mind and gods and angels and souls and soul mates and
jesusallahmoseskrishnaoralrobertsspiritualityradicalhonestyan-
dotherhorseshitforevermorerightandwronggoodandbadupand-
downsmartanddumbdualismandnondualismetc — and thousands
of other zippy little radio-San-Juan-rock-and-roll-shows-of-the-
mind, chattering away, day and night, on and on. Those are called
memes, and what a cruel joke they are! A big proportion of this last
section of this book is about memes, and it pretty much covers all
of that horseshit about belief in one swell poop.

I, personally, as a Futilitarian, don't believe in anything anymore. Actually I do. I have one religious belief that I hold on to, in
hopes of crowding out all the others. Pygmies are stealing my lug-
gage. I stole that belief from the great novelist Saul Bellow. I believe
it. My golf clubs got stolen from an airplane not to long ago and this
reconfirmed my faith in my religion and my faith in humanity at
the same time. I thought immediately of the one belief I knew I
could depend on: "I knew it! Can't trust those pygmies!" Here is
how you graduate from ignorance to dumbness: give up believing

in belief. That leads directly to liberation from the jail of the mind, and then to profound social transformation.

What? What does futilitarianism about belief have to do with the transformation of human society? Social Transformation has to do with telling the truth about what you notice — particularly what you notice in your mind right now. Culture lives in human minds. Culture is what is killing us. When you notice what is in your mind, you need to say it out loud so we can all examine it. When you report simply what you notice that seems to make sense to you and what doesn't, with detachment rather than righteousness, (given that it's all bullshit anyway) and say what you value, (more bullshit) it can be played with rather than guarded and preserved. This is useful and fun and leads to personal transformation. When you admit out loud that you are attached to something, you've really done something.

If you are dumb enough, you honestly report what you notice, as the thoughts appear. It is a practice like meditation. You have a sensation in your body and a thought in your mind at the same time. You report both. The sensation lets you know you are emotionally attached to the thought or interpretation. You wish to advocate something and/or to oppose something. You tell the truth about it, as descriptively as you can. What happens then is the possibility of freedom to actually choose in that moment rather than just continue the chain reaction you call your life, where you play like you are in charge even though you aren't.

Part Five, this section, is the story of a number of people who did just that. They told the truth about what they are attached to and value as descriptively as they could. The people who contributed these upcoming stories are brilliantly, incredibly, dumb. Transformation is getting from ignorance to dumbness.

The ongoing transformation of society occurs through the individual transformation of its participants, shared and thereby furthered. Each individual transformation is a threat to the existing social order. Each hero of honest noticing and reporting is a revolutionary. Common sense, from the renewed perspective of dumbness, heals us of the disease of being carried away by thought into never never land. Each new discovery of wisdom from individual liberation threatens the old order, and when it is shared it becomes an even greater threat. The cumulative effect of these heroes, whose stories are told in this book, will eventually bring about the evolution of the society of which they and we are a part.

There are more of us dummies doing this than most of us have imagined. We have known our numbers are growing and what we have in common for a long time, but we are just beginning to get a glimmer of the fact that there will soon be more of us than there are of them. The demonstrations all over the world against the proposed war on Iraq by the old order in the United States, in the winter and spring of 2003, were a sign of coming massive transformation. The dummies will one day soon outnumber the ignoramuses. Think of that. In a recent survey more people called themselves independents (35%) than Republicans (32%) or Democrats (31%). Something is happening with people's faith in the mental illness called moralism.

e. e. cummings, in 1938, described it this way:

"What their most synthetic not to mention transparent majesty, mrsandmr collective foetus, would improbably call a ghost is walking. He isn't an undream of anaesthetized impersons, or a cosmic-comfortstation, or a transcendentally sterilized lookiesoundiefeelie-tastiesmellie. He is a healthily complex, a naturally homogeneous, citizen of immortality. The now of his each pitying free imperfect gesture, his any breath or being, insults perfected inframortally millenniums of slavishness. He is a little more than everything, he is democracy, he is alive; he is ourselves." (From the Introduction to *New Poems*).

We have here at the end of this book more evidence that a ghost is walking. The ghost whispers that liberation from the mind jail is the key to our survival and enlightenment. Our intellect cannot save us he says, only our being, using our intellect, to share with other beings.

At the turn of the century in our culture it was all the rage to try to use the intellect to correct the fundamental nature of the human being, which was considered to be base and uncivilized. The fundamental nature of man to fundamentalists is that we are all hog-faced pleasure-seekers, rapists and murderers who need to be controlled or eliminated. What cummings advocated and what we advocate is just the reverse. We want to correct civilization's obsession with management, control, mass murder, commerce and rape of the earth and other displaced forms of disowned and lied-about aggression and sexuality. We want to do this by getting back to our more basic nature, which is to take care of each other, care for each other, share with each other, honor each other, take from each other, give to each other, work out ways of forgiving each other, get beyond categories of good and bad and right, wrong and into the experience of presence to each other. This is just as much a part of our basic nature as our sexuality or our aggression. We have limbic brains that are about caring and they are a more ancient part of our evolution than our frontal lobes. (See *Radical Parenting: Seven Steps to a Functional Family in a Dysfunctional World,* Chapter 12.)

And when we tell the truth about our aggression and sexuality in the form of honestly expressed resentment and appreciation, and we acknowledge our horniness and our various escapades like dummies who didn't know any better, everything changes. Our perspective changes. Our intellect gets corrected. We acknowledge what is true. We let the truth come in. We admit the truth.

To have our intellect constantly corrected by nature, our nature, by what is natural for us — for us to share, to tell each other what is so about our lives, about what our lives are like for us — is to bring about a new civilization! The more of us who have the courage to tell the truth as though we didn't know any better, the more we can change our lives and our world. This is the best hope we have for survival — heroes who tell the truth. This whole book is the recent evidence from our end of the block, and this last section is the biggest story of all.

Social Action and the Cutting Edge of the Science of Cognition and Creativity

We are dealing with social action, science and evolutionary theory all at the same time in this part of the book, because it is what we have to do in order to get the most inclusive perspective on honesty. This is the most difficult story to tell and it gets harder as we move toward the end of this book. It is difficult because it requires thinking, real thinking, hard thinking—and because it requires action from a perspective of disowning traditional wisdom and seeing it as merely cumulative human ignorance over time. Without the arrogance to call ourselves fools, all will be lost.

Some of the stories here become essays, because the biggest stories can only be told that way. They are based on one great big story—the story of what it is to be a human being. This is a story in which we all get to participate in the outcome. Though this is the hardest story to get it's the one that is by far the most rewarding. Once we have this story clear it is equally clear at exactly the same time that we must reform our institutions to reflect what we have learned.

My friend, Tom Atlee, author of *The Tao of Democracy* and founder of the Co-Intelligence Institute, said this in a recent letter: "...it is not enough for some of us (or even many of us) to know that something is a lie. We need institutional ways to clarify the lies and see more clearly COLLECTIVELY, in ways that are closely linked to our official decision-making processes. Right now we don't have that. For example, we need: (1) Campaign Finance reform; (2) Voting reform; and (3) citizen deliberative councils. (Can you imagine a group of two dozen randomly selected citizens interviewing candidates in depth for a day or two and then issuing their findings in voters information booklets? Or reviewing campaign ads before they're aired? Or passing judgment on legislation considered since the last election and rating legislative candidates according to how well their votes (real or proposed) aligned with the desires of the citizens — and then having those ratings printed right on the ballot?!) I think those three reforms are very synergistic and would pretty much do the trick fixing up the election part of our democracy..."

So here it comes, the big story of how we become co-intelligent. All of the stories in this final section are about that, the biggest human story of all — about how we build institutions to become on-goingly co-intelligent and self-correcting, based on honesty.

The first one is about social action, covering the arrest and trial of citizens working for campaign finance reform. What follows is the story of memes and the work of Richard Dawson and Susan Blackmore. Then George Carlin chimes in with his hilarious and foul-mouthed memetic correction of patriotism and other 'isms'. And finally, there is a closing summation on the compassionate revolution and the inverse relationship between secrecy and human progress.

This conclusion to *The Truthtellers*, Sourcing a Way to Settle and Source Things Among the Settlements of Sorcerers, is the final box containing all the other boxes in the "boxes within boxes" para-digm with which this book was built. Personal honesty is the key to liberation from the solitary confinement of the individual mind, the jail of family, and the usual prison of work. An honest community of friends is the work release program for the inmates. And now, finally, comes the ongoing revision and upgrading of the whole court system, so that recidivism is minimized and the ex-cons are truly liberated and put in charge of the courts.

End of story.

28 Undoing a System of Secret Influence

W e called ourselves the Freedom Brigade. We were supported by a number of other people from The Alliance for Democracy. We were trying to keep alive the conversation about the way campaigns are financed in this country in an attempt to undo the lie that we have a democracy (rule by the people here) rather than a plutocracy (rule by only the wealthy people). There are about 20 or 30 industries that gave over 10 million dollars to campaigns in the last several elections, divided between the two political parties, in the so-called two party system, in order to control government legislation. We began by revealing all the information about campaign financing of both parties in detail with handouts, articles and personal conversations. We did all this to contribute to and expand the dialogue about campaign finance reform. In late 1999 and early 2000, we assembled in the Rotunda of the United States Capitol Building and made them arrest us, process us and try us in order to draw attention to the issue.

This chapter is reprinted, with some revisions, from *Honest to God: A Change of Heart That Can Change the World* by Brad Blanton and Neale Donald Walsch.

The conversations in the paddy wagon and in jail and in the courtroom showed that those of us who participated in this social action did so out of our own individual transformations and out of our compassion—out of our identification with other human beings. Because we had found out some things about who we were, both good and bad things, we understood more about how people can both be wonderful and be screwed up. We protested the screwedupness of the few who were hurting the many. We were protesting that some screwed up people have a lot more power than the rest of the screwed up people. We were for equal opportunity screwedupness—a thing called democracy. It ain't much, but it's better than the plutocracy we currently have.

A month or so after we were arrested and released, we went to trial. There, we learned more about the relationship between individual and social transformation.

In April of 2001, the McCain/Feingold campaign finance reform bill passed the Senate, fifteen months after the protests to bring it to public attention that are described here. What was proposed in that bill is still a far cry from full public financing. It only makes it a little harder for multi-national corporations to keep their bribes secret, and somewhat limits how much they can pay, but there are ways being worked out to get around it completely. Even that modest attempt at reform may never have any teeth, because of the degree of obligation members of both parties in Congress have to people who have paid for their election campaigns.

One important manifestation of spiritual growth is compassion in action. It is clear from peoples' testimonies that their willingness to act to change the laws about campaign financing is based on their own spiritual growth, and that compassion for others and love of their families is a central consideration.

I got arrested because I believe that there is a relationship between personal freedom from the mind and social freedom from domination by antiquated institutions. The protest my friends and I made was against secret alliances of institutions of influence to elect candidates. I wrote the article that follows because I thought that the testimony of all of us eloquently expressed a vital point of view. It also shows how individuals committed to having the truth be known can begin to hold the government accountable for being open and honest and telling the truth.

Criminal Justice: Hey! That's a Good Name for It!

The first arrests were in October of 1999 when Ronnie Dugger, founder of the Alliance for Democracy and seven others held up signs and spoke in loud voices in the Rotunda of the Capitol building in Washington about democracy being for sale. Then, six more of us got arrested in January, a part of the Democracy Brigade started by the Alliance for Democracy. We got arrested to protest the way campaigns are financed by multi-national corporations, giving them undue influence. That is called a plutocracy. We wanted that issue talked about and revealed to everyone in the country in hopes that democracy — another faulty, though more honest, form of government — might prevail.

We were arrested the first time, in 2000, in the last week in January. Then, a third Democracy Brigade made up of sixteen of us got arrested in the Rotunda again on February 29, leap year. In March most of the last arrest group went to trial — fourteen friends, all guilty of the same offense. (Two of our number couldn't make it to the first trial date set and had to get postponements to a later date.)

I was guilty. I pled guilty. But I didn't feel guilty. I had a hell of a good time being guilty. I fell in love with a bunch of people and felt real good about myself and I think most of us did too, and I want to tell you about it. It feels good to take a stand for the truth.

As each person's name was called out it seemed like a roll call of nationalities. We had last names that showed that our little jury box melting pot family was sourced from all over Europe, and several of us had blood in our veins from native America as well.

We all got to enter a plea of guilty and testify briefly about why we broke the law. What follows are excerpts from the transcript of the court record of our testimony, the judge's response and a bit of the story of what emerged. Freedom showed up. Democracy happened.

It was late in the day and the judge had been kind enough to have us seated in the empty jury box, rather than forcing all of us to remain standing while each person testified. The judge, a distinguished looking middle-aged, graying man, named Weissberg, had just addressed us personally, one at a time, asking us a series of questions. He asked each of us if we were sober, and not under the influence of drugs. He asked if we clearly understood that if we entered a plea of guilty we could get six months in prison and a $500 fine or both. We all said, one at a time, that we understood. Then we were allowed to testify. He asked us to try to keep it under two minutes.

When it came our turn to testify, each of us stood up when we spoke, and sat down again when we finished. We ranged in age from 18 to 76. Somehow in that controlled and formal setting, in that big hollow courtroom, and that great range of age, the words each of us spoke to account for why we were there, had a kind of declarative, definitive ring, and a cumulative effect, like an inscription on a tombstone.

Our attorney was polite but persistent (he wasn't in the American Civil Liberties Union for nothing). The judge, you could tell, was overloaded and a little tired, but happy to have a reprieve from much more boring work. Even the government prosecutor was actually paying attention to what we said. We "guilties" were all in love with each other for being brave enough to get there. When we listened to each other speak, some of us cried. Even the judge was moved by what we said. As we continued to speak, more and more clarity about what we were doing there seemed to emerge. These are only brief excerpts but they give some sense of what was said and what it was like to be there. I got to speak first because my last name starts with a B.

Superior Court of the District of Columbia

March 23, 2000

"Mr. Blanton?"

The Witness:

I'm Dr. Brad Blanton. I'm the author of a book called *Radical Honesty*. I have been a Clinical Psychologist in Washington, D.C. for the last twenty-five years. I'm demonstrating in the Capitol against campaign finance corruption in protest of the way the world economic order works.

If we were to take the whole population of the world and reduce it to a group of 100 people in a room, with all ratios remaining the same, 80 of them would be ill-housed, 50 of them would be suffering from malnutrition and illnesses related to malnutrition, 70 of them would be functionally unable to read, one would have a college degree, one would own a computer, and six of them would control enough of the resources to essentially control all the rest of the people in the room. All six of the rich people would be citizens of the United States of America.

It seems to me that if we were, in fact, in a room with 100 people and we got to know each other; see each other, talk to each other, smell each other and hear each other, we would probably get these problems handled — because normal human compassion would come into effect after people actually experienced each other. But with over six billion people on the planet, what maintains the conditions that keep these circumstances in place is something called the primary valuing of the bottom line. The people who have the money can afford to buy the legislation necessary to do just that — maintain the bottom line as a primary value. They do that through financing campaigns for people elected to public office and by constantly influencing them with paid lobbyists.

So campaign finance reform to me is critical to being actually compassionate rather than some kind of phony compassion that's part of the current political dialogue. So I'm proud to plead guilty. I am guilty as charged for demonstrating in the Capitol Rotunda against campaign finance corruption."

"Mr. Conant?"

"We did not risk arrest lightly, but from the sense that to speak truth to power in the Capitol was our civic responsibility, an action not disrespectful for our country, but rather undertaken from a profound love of it—from the passionate love of the principles on which it was founded and out of the deep fear that these principles are increasingly subverted by the corrupt system which makes Congress far more responsive to the needs of corporate donors than to the people."

"Ms. Cusimano?"

"I would like to pass on a better way of voting for my daughter and children."

"Mr. Cusimano?"

"My family, my friends and neighbors, voting members of our nation have lost faith in our representation of our Government. True statesmen are left out of the political arena, along with the people's concerns, needs and desires. We, the people, want our Government back. We, the people, want our country, our democracy back for ourselves and for our children."

"Mr. Demere?"

"Your Honor, I have ten grand children. I'm concerned about their future, the kind of nation they will inherit. The power of money that exerts pressure on politicians eats away at the health of our society. Behind many of our social ills lies the infamous influence of big money on the affairs of state."

When Mr. Demere the elder sat down, his son David was called upon.

"Mr. David Demere?"

"One of his ten grandchildren (nodding at his father), is my daughter who's now 17, Laquisha Demere, and I named her in honor of Laquisha Mott, whose statue is there in the Rotunda. I brought my daughter there seven years ago to look at that sculpture. I named her Laquisha because I wanted her to have the same kind of conviction that Laquisha Mott had for justice and fairness and equality. That is why I stood in the shadow of Laquisha Mott in the Rotunda with the other 16 activists there, acting out of conscience in an effort to expose and change the corporate oriented, big money campaign system we have in our beloved country."

"Mr. Hanmann?"

"That great domed space is replete with pictures and sculptures of history and heroes; it is presumed to be a museum. But when I entered the Rotunda on February 29th, I thought I was on the stage of democracy. I misbehaved in the museum of our history in order to confront our future. So the Rotunda was for me a platform, a stage on which I sought redress of my grievances and where I claimed the right of free expression and free speech at the very hub of government... there to protest that political commerce that displaces a government of ordinary people with the government of special money."

"Ms. Kenler?"

"Your Honor, I have just a bit of hope left that the state of our earth and the health of all the creatures on it can be helped by our actions. And I really do believe that full public financing of campaigns could bring about what most people want, which is a good life, and this is the best I can do to take that responsibility for myself and for my family and my community."

"Mr. McMichael?"

"We know that unless they're restrained in the political employment of their wealth, experience shows that the wealthy will come to dominate the society to the great detriment of the non-wealthy, who in all societies, are the great majority."

"Ms. Parry?"

"I do not come here lightly. I do not want to be here. Nor did I want to have to demonstrate in the Capitol Rotunda. I had no wish to be arrested. I went to the Rotunda on February 29th to redress my grievances with Congress because they are not listening and the media is not reporting. I went, Your Honor, because I believe in my deepest of hearts that our democracy is at stake."

"Mr. Price?"

"Unless I openly state my grievances against the democracy killing effects of corporate money in the legislative and electoral processes, I will have, through my silence, negated the sacrifices of democracy's heroes, including those of my father who served in Germany in World War II."

"Mr. Silver?"

"I think the folks here have summed it up. This is the reform that has to happen in order to make any other reform possible. And it's the only issue I would do this for. And I do it with great pride."

"Mr. Stanton?"

"In 1931, April Crawford and Arnold Stanton came to Washington, D.C. from North Carolina to get married. They got married in the Washington Monument. They believed in this country. They believed in democracy. They had hopes. Almost 70 years later, I come to the Rotunda, their son, because I have to speak out because I feel like my democracy has gone. A lot has happened in those 70 years. Most of what has happened has done more and more to disenfranchise us. I don't want my grandsons to come here and do the sort of things I did at this time to get attention to get the government back to the beat."

After Mr. Stanton, the judge took his turn to speak. This is just my opinion, but I think he was aware that he was speaking into a listening created by us, and that it was a listening worth speaking into, and that he wanted to actually thank us for being who we were.

"I took guilty pleas yesterday or the day before from a much smaller group, I think four people who were demonstrating for a different cause under slightly different circumstances. And I used the opportunity to engage them, as I could, about what it was they were here for and who they were when they were not here. And to some extent, to debate them about some issues that I felt were relevant—although not on the merits of their cause. I would enjoy the opportunity to do that with you folks because you are all obviously very passionate about what you believe in and committed to this issue, and also very articulate in expressing your point of view.

"And if this were a different forum and if time permitted it, I think I would enjoy the intellectual stimulation of getting to know you better and maybe even playing devils' advocate on some issues. But I think that would be self-indulgent on my part at this point. And it's late and I don't think we can do that.

"It seems to me the sentence suggested by your attorney is a fair one. You've spent five hours of some indignity paying a price for doing what you did, and I don't see any need to exact a higher penalty. Although there is an addition to that: a cost of $50 which is obligatory... mandatory under the statute for the Victims of Violent Crime Compensation Fund which every person convicted has to contribute to, so that people who are victimized by crime and cannot afford to pay the cost of their injury, can have some fund to draw on to help defray those costs. So that's what I intend to do.

"The only thing I would add is something that I talked about the other day with the other four. And that is that what I'm not sure of as a judge, and I've been doing this a long time, and I've also dealt with a lot of, if I can use the term, demonstrator arrests or demonstration arrests. But what I haven't really thought through clearly in my own mind is whether there should be an escalating price if someone's conscience compels them to come back again and again and we have to drop everything and conduct court for them as we do. Whether there's a rule for deterrence and whether it's even a proper consideration for sentencing in court for a criminal act such as this.

"I don't know how I'll resolve that, but I state it only as sort of a something for you to think about. And maybe as a warning because all of you are obviously so passionate about what you believe in that there may well come a time, whether on this issue or some other issue, your conscience will bring you back to Washington in some other form of demonstration and there will be another arrest. And if there is, if the judge before whom you appear feels that the proper thing to do, having gotten essentially a—I don't mean this in a demeaning way—but having gotten essentially a free pass the first time, there should be a higher price to pay the second time, then you should prepare yourselves for that.

"Because you all know and one of the reasons I'm required by law to ask you about it before I take your plea is that when you do this sort of thing, the maximum price you could be asked to pay would be six months in jail or a $500 fine, or both. And that is a very steep price and one needs to know that before they decide how to conduct their affairs.

"Having said that, the sentence for all 14 of you is what I'll call time served, which is intended to reflect the five hours that you were held before you were released and a requirement that you pay $50 to the Victims of Violent Crime Compensation Fund, which is payable in the finance office in Room 4203.

"Thank you. You can all be excused. You will have to wait until we give you this form which you take with you to pay the $50 in the finance office and then you're free to leave."

We appreciated him for what he said. We liked him. He liked us. The truth is, even in that sterile place, in that stale and antiquated system, that completely deadened context where the dead law usually bores people to tears, for the time being, for the moment, at least, a spirit of compassion was around. Everyone in the room had been touched by each other's presence and each other's words and we were in a place of community and we were happy—and the judge just couldn't leave after we were through! And we didn't want to leave either! He stayed and talked with us for 20 minutes after the trial was over and was, I believe, actually honored to be with us.

Another Day, Another Judge

A week or so later, one of our colleagues, who couldn't make it to court with us that day, got another judge on another day, who did not allow her to testify on her own behalf whatsoever, and sentenced her to 5 days in jail and the maximum $500 fine. That penalty was for the same offense we had committed, right beside her, on the same day, at the same time.

There are two things you can say about the courts and the criminal justice system: (1) What happens to you still mostly depends on the judge you get and the mood they are in; and (2) The Criminal Justice System is well named.

Commitment to changing the arbitrariness of that system clearly has to be part of what we who are interested in honesty and fairness are about.

The judge our group had was an exception, and stood out because of it. The judge our friend got was pretty much just doing her job as a hireling of the corporate status quo which we were protesting in the first place.

In the transcript of our trial the court reporter kept substituting the word "conscious" for the word "conscience" spoken by the judge, and the mistake was more than just entertaining. I think consciousness requires that we transcend the limitations of the law and the courts by choosing how we behave independently, and separate from the system, and that we do not cooperate with it out of fear. Somehow we have to learn how to be able to love a bad judge, in a bad mood, on a bad day, without honoring a dishonorable system. Come to think of it, that is pretty much the same thing it takes for most of us to get along with each other and ourselves about half the time anyway. To love the being I am, in spite of my mind, is why I meditate. That seems a direct analogy to loving a variety of judges in a variety of moods but not honoring the crap they come up with in the slightest.

Compassion for ourselves and compassion for others must be achieved independently from the "shoulds" of our individual minds and the bad laws and systems of society. It has to be worked out in the heart and in the world through honest self-expression and a change of heart. We have to raise Hell and fight and yell and write until we can work through to a place of forgiveness of others and ourselves in order to have the power to change the world. So I am going back to the Capitol Rotunda again to learn some more about that. Individual transformation and social transformation can't really be separated. You can't have one without the other.

We were lucky this time—most of us. We got a good judge on a good day this time around. We got a chance to speak up and make our point get to know each other and publish this story. And we got off with just "time served." Maybe we'll be lucky again. Who knows?

This appears to be how social change occurs: Everyone gets busted, including not just us who have the papers to show for it, but also the cops, the court system, the politicians, the business-people, the lobbyists and those of you who haven't shown up yet. Getting busted and acknowledging it is the first step toward getting over old models of the mind. Old models of the mind that don't fit reality anymore, on the individual human level, are called ignorance, and are the source of suffering. Old models of the mind that don't fit reality anymore on the social level are called tradition, heritage, necessity, or the law, and are also the source of suffering. The very tough process of getting mad and getting over it, or getting hurt and getting over it, getting busted and getting over it, being treated unfairly and getting over it, is necessary, so that antiquated systems of thought and governance can be dispensed with. It is called forgiveness. Forgiveness leads to compassion and vice versa. Compassion leads to freedom. Lucky for us, there is a lot to forgive out there.

The process itself may require telling a judge to go to Hell somewhere along the way, or a corporation to dissolve, but that's what we created a democratic society for in the first place, wasn't it? I think we are all learning, individually and together. I think we will, someday soon, have justice prevail and compassion win out and forgiveness become possible. I can see us all marching down the corridors of justice, singing about the simultaneity of individual and social transformation..."you can't have one, no you can't have none, you can't have one without the o-o-other." Most people probably won't know what in the Hell we are singing about, but it is a big part of our job to tell them until they get it. Individual transformation and social transformation happen at the same time.

29

Solving the World's Problems by Any Memes Possible: The Story About Stories

We are evolving. We are beginning to see that we are a part of something much bigger than ourselves. If we think of ourselves as aligned with something that is bigger than us, we can ask some questions about how that which is greater than us operates. We can think of ourselves as observers of the larger forces within which we live and engage in a dialogue from that perspective. For example, we can give evolution a voice. This is what people who invented God were attempting to do, but as we know, it is dangerous, because people start believing concepts are real, then get lost in ideas and ideals very easily. The usefulness of reification of a process for the sake of dialogue, is however, still useful if we don't start believing in our beliefs as though they were real, but just use them as models for discovery.

One of the most vexing questions the process of evolution has to answer is: "What is to be done with human beings?" In the ongoing course of natural selection, the current problem of evolving life on earth centers around the question of whether we humans are to be eliminated, or, if not, how we might participate in evolution consciously.

We are not necessary for the evolution of life to continue. But is there any way we can remain ourselves as participants and even help ourselves along by consciously taking on the task of cooperating with evolution and even having a say in its direction? Can our consciousness, which has evolved to the point where it might be useful as well as destructive to the process, help by participating in the flow in some way that honors the flow itself? Can we participate in the complex and beautiful flow of life on earth and in the universe and influence its direction to serve life, and also ourselves, rather than either one or the other?

To think deeply as conscious participants in the process of evolution we must begin with an understanding of (1) natural selection, an idea we humans have been playing with for 142 years, (and it is about to soak in); and (2) memes, a new analog to genetics in the world of thought, that has only been around for twenty years or so. After getting that understanding, the perspective of the gene meme and the perspective of the meme meme, it will become clear that to have any chance of conscious participation with evolution we must (3) invent some way to depend on each other implicitly with a high level of certainty that we can trust each other. (We must do that because we have to think with more than one brain at a time now, and we have to notice with more than one sensorium!) How to do that (get to where we can be sure we can depend on each other) is the primary focus of this document and the two projects described at the end of this story.

There is no better place to begin this discussion than to read the following brilliant article by Dr. Susan Blackmore, "Waking from the Meme Dream," which is reproduced in whole here because to excerpt from it would possibly reduce it's clarity. Susan Blackmore is the author of *The Meme Machine* (Oxford

Press, 1998), which is an even more elaborate and brilliant articulation of what we get a taste of in this presentation.

Waking from the Meme Dream*

Wake up! Wake up!

Errrr, ummmm, grrrrggr, Oh yes, I'm awake now. Wow, that was a weird dream. I really thought I had to escape from the slurb, and it mattered terribly to get to the cupboard in time. How silly! Of course, now I see it wasn't real at all.

Wake up! Wake up!

What do you mean, "Wake up," I'm already awake. This is real. This does matter.

I can't wake up any more. Go away!

Wake up! Wake up!

But I don't understand—from what? And how?

These are the questions I want to tackle today. From what are we to awaken? And how? My answers will be "From the meme dream" and "By seeing that it is a meme dream." But it may take me some time to explain!

There is a long history, in spiritual and religious traditions, of the idea that normal waking life is a dream or illusion. This makes no sense to someone who looks around and is convinced there is a real world out there and a self who perceives it. However, there are many clues that this ordinary view is false. Some clues come from spontaneous mystical experiences in which people "see the light!," realize that everything is one, and go "beyond self" to see the world "as it really is." They feel certain that the new way of seeing is better and truer than the old (though of course they could be mistaken!).

Other clues come from spiritual practice. Probably the first thing that anybody discovers when they try to meditate, or be

*This paper was presented at: The Psychology of Awakening: International Conference on Buddhism, Science and Psychotherapy, in Dartington, 7-10 November 1996, by Susan Blackmore, Department of Psychology, University of the West of England, Bristol BS16 2JP.

mindful, is that their mind is constantly full of thoughts. Typically these are not wise and wonderful thoughts, or even useful and productive thoughts, but just endless chatter. From the truly trivial to the emotionally entangling, they go on and on. And what's more they nearly all involve "me." It is a short step to wondering who this suffering self is, and why "I" can't stop the thoughts.

Finally clues come from science. The most obvious (and scary) conclusion from modern neuroscience is that there is simply no one inside the brain. The more we learn about the way the brain functions the less it seems to need a central controller, a little person inside, a decider of decisions or an experiencer of experiences. These are just fictions—part of the story the brain tells itself about a self within (Churchland and Sejnowski, 1992; Dennett, 1991).

Some say there is no point in striving for an intellectual understanding of spiritual matters. I disagree. It is true that intellectual understanding is not the same as realization, but this does not mean it is useless. In my own tradition of practice, Zen, there is much room for intellectual struggle; for example, in the cultivation of the "don't know mind," or in working with koans. You can bring a question to such a state of intellectual confusion that it can be held, poised, in all its complexity and simplicity. Like "Who am I?" "What is this?" or (one I have struggled with) "What drives you?"

There is also a terrible danger in refusing to be intellectual about spiritual matters. That is, we may divorce our spiritual practice from the science on which our whole society depends. If this society is going to have any spiritual depths to it, they must fit happily with our growing understanding of the workings of the brain and the nature of mind. We cannot afford to have one world in which scientists understand the mind, and another in which special people become enlightened.

So I make no apologies for my approach. I am going to try to answer my questions using the best science I can find. We seem to live in a muddle that we think matters to a self that doesn't exist. I want to find out why.

Darwin's Dangerous Idea

There is one scientific idea, which, to my mind, excels all others. It is exquisitely simple and beautiful. It explains the origins of all life forms and all biological design. It does away with the need for God, for a designer, for a master plan or for a purpose in life. Only in the light of this idea does anything in biology make sense. It is, of course, Darwin's idea of evolution by natural selection.

The implications of natural selection are so profound that people have been awe-struck or maddened; fascinated or outraged, since it was first proposed in *The Origin of Species* in 1859. This is why Dennett (1995) calls it Darwin's Dangerous Idea. Sadly, many people have misunderstood the idea and, even worse, have used it to defend indefensible political doctrines which have nothing to do with Darwinism. I therefore hope you will forgive me if I spend some time explaining it as clearly as I can.

All you need for natural selection to get started is a replicator in an appropriate environment. A replicator is something that copies itself, though not always perfectly. The environment must be one in which the replicator can create numerous copies of itself, not all of which can survive. That's it.

Can it really be that simple? Yes. All that happens is this — in any one copying generation, not all the copies are identical and some are better able to survive in that environment than others are. In consequence they make more copies of themselves and so that kind of copy becomes more numerous. Of course things then begin to get complicated. The rapidly expanding population of copies starts to change the environment and that changes the selective pressures. Local variations in the environment mean different kinds of copy will do well in different places and so more complexity arises. This way the process can produce all the kinds of organized complexity we see in the living world — yet all it needs is this one simple, elegant, beautiful, and obvious process — natural selection.

To make things more concrete let's imagine a primeval soup in which a simple chemical replicator has arisen. We'll call the replicators "Blobbies." These blobbies, by virtue of their chemical constitution, just do make copies of themselves whenever they find the right chemicals. Now, put them in a rich chemical swamp and they start copying, though with occasional errors. A few million years go by and there are lots of kinds of blobbies. The ones that need lots of swampon have used up all the supplies and are failing, so now the sort that can use isoswampin instead, are doing better. Soon there are several areas in which different chemicals predominate and different kinds of blobby appear. Competition for swamp chemicals gets fierce and most copies that are made die out. Only those that, by rare chance, turn out to have clever new properties, go on to copy themselves again.

Clever properties might include the ability to move around and find the swampon, to trap isoswampin and hang onto it, or to build a membrane around themselves. Once blobbies with membranes appear, they will start winning out over free-floating ones and super-blobbies are made.

Another few million years go by and tricks are discovered like taking other blobbies inside the membrane, or joining several super-blobbies together. Super-dooper-blobbies appear, like multi-celled animals with power supplies and specialized parts for moving about and protecting themselves. However, these are only food to even bigger super-dooper-blobbies. It is only a matter of time before random variation and natural selection will create a vast living world. In the process billions and billions of unsuccessful blobbies have been created and died, but such a slow, blind process produces the goods. "The goods" on our planet includes bacteria and plants, fish and frogs, duck-billed platypuses and us.

Design appears out of nothing. There is no need for a creator or a master plan, and no end point towards which creation is heading. Richard Dawkins (1996) calls it "Climbing Mount Improbable." It is just a simple but inexorable process by which unbelievably improbable things get created.

It is important to remember that evolution has no foresight and so doesn't necessarily produce the "best" solution. Evolution can only go on from where it is now. That is why, among other things, we have such a daft design in our eyes, with all the neurons going out of the front of the retina and getting in the way of the light. Once evolution had started off on this kind of eye it was stuck with it. There was no creator around to say "hey, start again with that one, let's put the wires out the back." Nor was there a creator around to say "Hey, let's make it fun for the humans." The genes simply do not care.

Understanding the fantastic process of natural selection we can see how our human bodies came to be the way they are. But what about our minds? Evolutionary psychology does not easily answer my questions.

For example, why do we think all the time? From a genetic point of view this seems extremely wasteful—and animals that waste energy don't survive. The brain uses about 20% of the body's energy while weighing only 2%. If we were thinking useful thoughts, or solving relevant problems there might be some point, but mostly we don't seem to be. So why can't we just sit down and not think?

Why do we believe in a self that does not exist? Someone may yet explain this in evolutionary terms, but at least superficially it appears pointless. Why construct a false idea of self, with all its mechanisms protecting self-esteem and its fear of failure and loss, when from the biological point of view it is the body that needs protecting. Note that if we thought of ourselves as the entire organism there would be no problem, but we don't—rather, we seem to believe in a separate self; something that is in charge of the body; something that has to be protected for its own sake. I bet if I asked you "Which would you rather lose—your body or your mind?" you wouldn't spend long deciding.

Like many other scientists I would love to find a principle as simple, as beautiful and as elegant as natural selection that would explain the nature of the mind.

I think there is one. It is closely related to natural selection. Although it has been around for twenty years, it has not yet been put fully to use. It is the theory of memes.

A Brief History of the Meme Meme

In 1976 Richard Dawkins wrote what is probably the most popular book ever on evolution: The Selfish Gene. The book gave a catchy name to the theory that evolution proceeds entirely for the sake of the selfish replicators. That is, evolution happens not for the good of the species, nor for the good of the group, nor even for the individual organism. It is all for the good of the genes. Genes that are successful spread and those that aren't don't. The rest is all a consequence of this fact.

Of course the main replicator he considered was the gene—a unit of information coded in the DNA and read out in protein synthesis. However, at the very end of the book he claimed that there is another replicator on this planet; the meme.

The meme is a unit of information (or instruction for behavior) stored in a brain and passed on by imitation from one brain to another. Dawkins gave as examples; ideas, tunes, scientific theories, religious beliefs, clothes fashions, and skills, such as new ways of making pots or building arches.

The implications of this idea are staggering and Dawkins spelt some of them out. If memes are really replicators then they will, inevitably, behave selfishly. That is, ones that are good at spreading will spread and ones that are not will not. As a consequence the world of ideas—or memosphere—will not fill up with the best, truest, most hopeful or helpful ideas, but with the survivors. Memes are just survivors like genes.

In the process of surviving they will, just like genes, create mutually supportive meme groups. Remember the blobbies. In a few million years they began to get together into groups, because the ones in groups survived better than loners. The groups got bigger and better, and a complex ecosystem evolved. In the real world of biology, genes have grouped together to create enormous creatures that then mate and pass the groups on. In a similar way memes may group together in human brains and fill the world of ideas with their products.

If this view is correct, then the memes should be able to evolve quite independently of the genes (apart from needing a brain). There have been many attempts to study cultural evolution, but most of them implicitly treat ideas (or memes) as subservient to the genes (see e.g. Cavalli-Sforza and Feldman, 1981; Crook, 1995; Durham, 1991; Lumsden and Wilson, 1981). The power of realizing that memes are replicators is that they can be seen as working purely and simply in their own interest. Of course to some extent memes will be successful if they are useful to their hosts, but this is not the only way for a meme to survive—and we shall soon see some consequences of this.

Since he first suggested the idea of memes Dawkins has discussed the spread of such behaviors as wearing baseball caps back to front (my kids have recently turned theirs the right way round again!), the use of special clothing markers to identify gangs, and (most famously) the power of religions. Religions are, according to Dawkins (1993), huge co-adapted meme-complexes; that is groups of memes that hang around together for mutual support and thereby survive better than lone memes could do. Other meme-complexes include cults, political systems, alternative belief systems, and scientific theories and paradigms.

Religions are special because they use just about every meme-trick in the book (which is presumably why they last so long and infect so many brains). Think of it this way. The idea of hell is initially useful because the fear of hell reinforces socially desirable behavior. Now add the idea that unbelievers go to hell, and the meme and any companions are well protected. The idea of God is a natural companion meme, assuaging fear and providing (spurious) comfort. The spread of the meme-complex is aided by exhortations to convert others and by tricks such as the celibate priesthood. Celibacy is a disaster for genes, but will help spread memes since a celibate priest has more time to spend promoting his faith.

Another trick is to value faith and suppress the doubt that leads every child to ask difficult questions like "where is hell?" and "If God is so good why did those people get tortured?" Note that science (and some forms of Buddhism) do the opposite and encourage doubt.

Finally, once you've been infected with these meme-complexes they are hard to get rid of. If you try to throw them out, some even protect themselves with last-ditch threats of death, ex-communication, or burning in hell-fire for eternity.

I shouldn't get carried away. The point I want to make is that these religious memes have not survived for centuries because they are true, because they are useful to the genes, or because they make us happy. In fact, I think they are false and are responsible for the worst miseries in human history. No—they have survived because they are selfish memes and are good at surviving—they need no other reason.

Once you start to think this way a truly frightening prospect opens up. We have all become used to thinking of our bodies as biological organisms created by evolution. Yet we still like to think of our selves as something more. We are in charge of our bodies, we run the show, we decide which ideas to believe in and which to reject. But do we really? If you begin to think about selfish memes it becomes clear that our ideas are in our heads because they are successful memes.

American philosopher Dan Dennett (1995) concludes that a "person" is a particular sort of animal infested with memes. In other words you and I and all our friends are the products of two blind replicators, the genes and the memes.

I find these ideas absolutely stunning. Potentially we might be able to understand all of mental life in terms of the competition between memes, just as we can understand all biological life in terms of the competition between genes.

What I want to do now, finally, is apply the ideas of memetics to the questions I asked at the beginning. What are we waking up from and how do we do it? Why is my head so full of thoughts?

This question has a ridiculously easy answer once you start thinking in terms of memes. If a meme is going to survive it needs to be safely stored in a human brain and passed accurately on to more brains. A meme that buries itself deep in the memory and never shows itself again will simply fizzle out. A meme that gets terribly distorted in the memory or in transmission, will also fizzle out. One simple way of ensuring survival is for a meme to get itself repeatedly rehearsed inside your head.

Take two tunes. One of them is tricky to sing, and even harder to sing silently to yourself. The other is a catchy little number that you almost can't help humming to yourself. So you do. It goes round and round. Next time you feel like singing aloud this tune is more likely to be picked for the singing. And if anyone is listening they'll pick it up too. That's how it became successful, and that's why the world is so full of awful catchy tunes and advertising jingles. But there is another consequence. Our brains get full up with them too. These successful memes hop from person to person, filling up their hosts' minds as they go. In this way all our minds get fuller and fuller.

We can apply the same logic to other kinds of meme. Ideas that go round and round in your head will be successful. Not only will they be well remembered, but when you are next talking to someone they will be the ideas "on your mind" and so will get passed on. They may get to this position by being emotionally charged, exciting, easily memorable or relevant to your current concerns. It does not matter how they do it. The point is that memes that get themselves repeated will generally win out over ones that don't.

The obvious consequence of this fact is that your head will soon fill up with ideas. Any attempt to clear the mind just creates spare processing capacity for other memes to grab.

This simple logic explains why it is so hard for us to sit down and "not think;" why the battle to subdue "our" thoughts is doomed. In a very real sense they are not "our" thoughts at all. They are simply the memes that happen to be successfully exploiting our brain-ware at the moment.

This raises the tricky question of who is thinking or not thinking. Who is to do battle with the selfish memes? In other words, who am I?

Who am I?

I suppose you can tell by now what my answer to this one is going to be. We are just co-adapted meme-complexes. We, our precious, mythical "selves", are just groups of selfish memes that have come together by and for themselves. This is a truly startling idea and, in my experience, the better you understand it, the more fascinating and weird it becomes. It dismantles our ordinary way of thinking about ourselves and raises bizarre questions about the relationship of ourselves to our ideas. To understand it we need to think about how and why memes get together into groups at all.

Just as with blobbies or genes, memes in groups are safer than free-floating memes. An idea that is firmly embedded in a meme-complex is more likely to survive in the memosphere than is an isolated idea. This may be because ideas within meme-groups get passed on together (e.g. when someone is converted to a faith, theory or political creed), get mutual support (e.g. if you hate the free-market economy you are likely also to favor a generous welfare state), and they protect themselves from destruction. If they did not, they would not last and would not be around today. The meme-complexes we come across are all the successful ones!

Like religions, astrology is a successful meme-complex. The idea that Leos get on well with Aquarians is unlikely to survive on its own, but as part of astrology is easy to remember and pass on.

Astrology has obvious appeal that gets it into your brain in the first place; it provides a nice (though spurious) explanation for human differences and a comforting (though false) sense of predictability. It is easily expandable (you can go on adding new ideas forever!) and is highly resistant to being overturned by evidence. In fact the results of hundreds of experiments show that the claims of astrology are false but this has apparently not reduced belief in astrology one bit (Dean, Mather and Kelly, 1996). Clearly, once you believe in astrology it is hard work to root out all the beliefs and find alternatives. It may not be worth the effort. Thus we all become unwitting hosts to an enormous baggage of useless and even harmful meme-complexes.

One of those is myself.

Why do I say that the self is a meme-complex? Because it works the same way as other meme-complexes. As with astrology, the idea of "self" has a good reason for getting installed in the first place. Then once it is in place, memes inside the complex are mutually supportive, can go on being added to almost infinitely, and the whole complex is resistant to evidence that it is false.

First the idea of self has to get in there. Imagine a highly intelligent and social creature without language. She will need a sense of self to predict others' behavior (Humphrey, 1986) and to deal with ownership, deception, friendships and alliances (Crook, 1980). With this straightforward sense of self she may know that her daughter is afraid of a high-ranking female and take steps to protect her, but she does not have the language with which to think "I believe that my daughter is afraid ... etc." It is with language that the memes really get going—and with language that "I" appears. Lots of simple memes can then become united as "my" beliefs, desires and opinions.

As an example, let's consider the idea of sex differences in ability. As an abstract idea (or isolated meme) this is unlikely to be a winner. But get it into the form "I believe in the equality of the sexes" and it suddenly has the enormous weight of "self" behind it.

"I" will fight for this idea as though I were being threatened. I might argue with friends, write opinion pieces, or go on marches. The meme is safe inside the haven of "self" even in the face of evidence against it. "My" ideas are protected.

Then they start proliferating. Ideas that can get inside a self — that is, be "my" ideas, or "my" opinions, are winners. So we all get lots of them. Before we know it, "we" are a vast conglomerate of successful memes. Of course there is no "I" who "has" the opinions. That is obviously a nonsense when you think clearly about it. Yes, of course there is a body that says "I believe in being nice to people" and a body that is (or is not) nice to people, but there is not in addition a self who "has" the belief.

Now we have a radically new idea of who we are. We are just temporary conglomerations of ideas, molded together for their own protection. The analogy with our bodies is close. Bodies are the creations of temporary gene-complexes: although each of us is unique, the genes themselves have all come from previous creatures and will, if we reproduce, go on into future creatures. Our minds are the creations of temporary meme-complexes: although each of us is unique, the memes themselves have come from previous creatures and will, if we speak and write and communicate, go on into future creatures. That's all.

The problem is that we don't see it this way. We believe there really is someone inside to do the believing, and really someone who needs to be protected. This is the illusion — this is the meme-dream from which we can wake up.

Dismantling the Meme-Dream

There are two systems I know of that are capable of dismantling meme-complexes (though I am sure there are others). Of course these systems are memes themselves but they are, if you like, meme-disinfectants, meme-eating memes, or "meme-complex destroying meme-complexes." These two are science and Zen.

Science works this way because of its ideals of truth and seeking evidence. It doesn't always live up to these ideals, but in principle it is capable of destroying any untruthful meme-complex by putting it to the test, by demanding evidence, or by devising an experiment.

Zen does this too, though the methods are completely different. In Zen training every concept is held up to scrutiny, nothing is left uninvestigated, even the self who is doing the investigation is to be held up to the light and questioned, "Who are you?"

After about 15 years of Zen practice, and when reading *The Three Pillars* of Zen by Philip Kapleau, I began working with the koan "Who...?" The experience was most interesting and I can best liken it to watching a meme unzipping other memes. Every thought that came up in meditation was met with "Who is thinking that?" or "Who is seeing this?" or "Who is feeling that?" or just "Who...?" Seeing the false self as a vast meme-complex seemed to help — for it is much easier to let go of passing memes than of a real, solid and permanent self. It is much easier to let the meme-unzipper do its stuff if you know that all it's doing is unzipping memes.

Another koan of mine fell to the memes. Q. "Who drives you?" A. "The memes of course." This isn't just an intellectual answer, but a way into seeing yourself as a temporary passing construction. The question dissolves when both self and driver are seen as memes.

I have had to take a long route to answer my questions but I hope you can now understand my answers. "From what are we to awaken?" From the meme dream of course. "And how?" "By seeing that it is a meme dream."

And who lets the meme-unzipper go its way? Who wakes up when the meme-dream is all dismantled? Ah, there's a question.

30

The Memonic Plague

There's a question, indeed. Who wakes up when the meme dream is all dismantled? Or I suppose we could say, "What wakes up when the meme dream is all dismantled?" We know something of a process of dismantling meme dreams called Radical Honesty, and we have observed differences between people pre- and post-dismantled meme complex. I think we have a clue as to what it is that is awakened. It is the noticer, who distinguishes noticing from thinking for a while. If one collects enough memories of noticing, one becomes identified as the observer primarily and can use that identity to focus on paying attention to paying attention in each moment. Thinking becomes secondary to noticing. However, in each instance of awakening one usually doesn't get to observe very long. The awakening is temporary. That which is awakened is soon overtaken again via infection with more meme complexes that include even the recent memory of the noticing, which hides actual noticing from view again, folding its new view of itself into a new meme complex, and the tale goes on. I will copy

Susan Blackmore now and take a longer route to 'splain that idea. The best start is the old Buddhist joke, "Hey! I'm awake!...Wasn't I!" or "Hey! I'm meditating! ...Wasn't I!"

Two Poems

I have written two poems in an attempt to serve here as a summary and a reminder of the ideas we have been pursuing here:

(1) Theme Song of the Categorically Ignorant

From genes and memes and dreams and schemes
And the fictions and predictions of the mind—
All together we're deluded
Into thinking we're included
In a plan—and we're in charge of the design

Since the day that we were born
In our flesh there's been a thorn
The insane idea of freedom is at large
To make us think someone who knows—
Is still in charge, and has on clothes—
And that there's more than piles of shit on this here barge.

But It turns out a human bean
Is just a big bullshit machine
We're just living in our stories
And inventing categories—
Mere expansions and contractions
Sensations and reactions
 Beliefs and interactions
Of the mind

These thoughts come—from God knows where
(If there was God and he was there)
 And we're all compelled to share
(Because in spite of thoughts we care)
The newest rage for what's in style
...in how to be.

But the cruelest thought of all,
Summer, winter, spring or fall
Is that we "think" that we're in charge
and that we're free.

Some of us have come to see
"Hey! There is no "self" inside of me!"
"So there's no one to be free!"
"Why you dirty S.O.B.!"
"Blame is just a game...
 to keep me in a dream that I that exist
...and that I'm free!"

From Gettysburg to old Antiedam,
You said we fought and died for freedom!
Well it's true we fought and died
As for the rest of it, you lied.
To create "unfree," then create "free,"
We must first create a "me!"
Then just to be, we cease to be, and that's called free.

I think it's a crying shame
And I'd like to find someone to blame
But it puts me back into the game
It puts ME back into the game
And I guess
it puts the game inside of me.

As long as we have a name
We live inside this game
of me and thee and we
and the struggle to be free
And it's the key
to how we...
who don't exist...
can cease to be.

The game's inside of me

Just as it is for thee
And we don't know how else to be.
Tee hee hee.

Question: What happens when something that doesn't exist ceases to be? The first answer is: Much ado about nothing.

Answer Two: The being, within which the something that doesn't exist resides, ceases to be, therefore it was killed by an illusion. The real being dies. The fictional self still doesn't exist. But now, neither does the being. You die for something that doesn't exist. You exist for something that doesn't die. Take the soldier who dies in a war, for example. A real being dies to preserve a meme.

(2) Roast 'Em, Toast 'Em, Siss Boom Bah!
An Ode To The Mind—Which Is Made Of Straa!

Looking through the prison's prism
I saw the gism from the ism schism
Squirming on the sidewalk there
without the grace of underwear.
And from the chance to see that ghost
I felt inspired to make a toast—

Here's to the cum of the scum of the earth!
To humanity's end that was there at it's birth!
To humanity!—whose primal soup for breakfast flowed into
a two martini Lunch with lobbyists, and after a brief nap,
came a supper of raw meat with an ocean of blood for a chaser...
and the party went on late into the night
until we ran out of each other to eat.

Here's to all us Not-see motherfuckers!
Here's to what our minds are most addicted to!
Fear and self-protection!
Hiding out in belief!
Religious arguments of right and wrong!
Here's to the meme of monotheism!

And to all its patriots and murderers and suicide bombers!

This one's on me!
And the next one's on you!
And all of them are on us!
In more ways than one!

The Withholding Memeplex

I have four books out now about radical honesty, the negative effects of lying and the liberating effects of sharing with others the truth of what one notices. They are all meme unzippers. The raw truth of what is noticed, shared without filtering or withholding, I call "radical honesty" to distinguish this simple descriptive form of reporting from the usual meme for honesty, which is some bullshit ideal or other, romanticized and idealized and tamed into be a thing of the mind for sentimentalistic preachers and soap opera watchers.

Radical honesty is the antidote to a very powerful meme complex in human beings—what we could call the "withholding for the sake of protecting meme." Withholding is a form of lying for the sake of protecting a set of illusions preserved in a guarded meme complex. The transcendent meme-complex-eating meme called "Radical Honesty" is about putting forth what you think, what you feel and what you have done, without qualification or inhibition, and let the memes fall where they may. It is in contrast to and in competition with "the withholding for the sake of protecting meme complex" which is commonly called "privacy" or "right to privacy" or "individual freedom," or various other better-sounding names.

One reason for advocating this alternative meme complex, "to reveal what is hidden," is that sharing openly allows for shared consciousness between people. That is, shared noticing and shared thinking. It increases the odds that one of us might be awake at the moment the rest of us are asleep and that they might wake the rest of us up. It also allows for (1) an ongoing correction of well copied but poorly fitting memes, as well as (2) poorly copied but better fitting memes. Noticing useful bad copies (new creative contexts or better-fit meme complexes) is the most fun, and the most active form of participating in our own social evolution.

The problem with what is kept secret is that it remains as an uncorrectable and isolated meme complex, hidden behind an agreed upon conspiracy of secrecy. The "isolation" or "withholding" meme can be copied and passed on and people can remain guarded and secretive and teach others to do the same in order to preserve memes like pickles. (That's why church ladies and conservatives look so prune-faced all the time.) Thus the memes within the withheld space never get corrected and can secretly mutate without being noticed, while being protected from exposure to a meme complex that might unzip them or make their replication become publicly modified. The faults of memes produced in isolation are never made conscious to the collective brains' meme complexes until something bad happens—so that correction of bad copies, or adaptation of incorrect copies can't be taken advantage of by either the originator of the errant copies or her fellow man.

As Susan Blackmore says, "'We' are a vast conglomerate of successful memes. Of course there is no 'I' who 'has' the opinions. That is obviously a nonsense when you think clearly about it. Yes, of course there is a body that says 'I believe in being nice to people' and a body that is (or is not) nice to people, but there is not in addition a self who 'has' the belief. "(*The Meme Machine*, Oxford, 1998) The illusion of the self is an operational fiction like the operational fiction called a meme.

Radical Honesty might be called a branch of the two meme-transcendent practices of Zen Buddhism and Science described by Susan Blackmore in her presentation. I couldn't agree more with her assertion that "We seem to live in a muddle that we think matters to a self that doesn't exist."

The very idea of a self, existing in isolation, and in need of being defended is undoubtedly something worth questioning. But who is to question it? I would like to call the questioners "the transcendent meme buddies," a meme complex of mutual meme complexes — the community of noticer-thinkers (rather than just thinkers) — the people who support each other to lead with noticing and follow with thinking, and then noticing again rather than the reverse. Traditionally this has been the ongoing discussion among existentialist philosophers and theologians for the last three or four hundred years, about Being vs. Doing. And resolving this conflict is what made Frank Sinatra, the greatest philosopher of the 20th Century. When he crooned "Do-be-do-be-do..." he came up with the answer. This is what the transcendent meme buddies do. They do and be and do and be together, zipping and unzipping meme complexes along the way.

A Summary Execution

What we notice is sensation and thought. We notice sensation and thought from the context of the meme complex called noticer/thinker. As a part of a community of noticer/thinkers with the usual modifications of perception associated with all memeplexes, we have a better chance of ongoing correction, modification and attempted upgrade for memes and memeplexes that better fit the environment. The environment includes the perceptual world, the meme world and the dreamed of possible world of the future. So our community environment, including memes and percepts, is not just the environment we are in together in the moment of noticing, it is also what we envision as possible together. This makes the meme environment different from the gene environment — we can think of possible things that don't exist yet and apply trial meme bad copies to it.

Radical honesty is a fundamental requirement for a community of noticer/thinkers to exist and evolve through conscious "partial meme management" through noticing and playing with the memestakes. We can participate on purpose and consciously in the modifications of the memes that run our lives if we don't waste a lot of time trying to preserve the old memeing in our lives, and if we spend a lot of time playing.

Lying is a problem of memes not being corrected by conscious human experience and consciously shared human interpretation. In particular, memes about what "should" be true, according to the thinker, often predominate over what is actually true according to the noticer. History is made up of stories of groups of thinkers with a vested interest in keeping alive their culture becoming more important than keeping alive. Thinking in isolation, without correction by noticing or by the community of noticer/thinkers eventually engenders grossly incorrect copies of very limited "should" memes. In fact, thinking, while withholding acknowledgment of what is there to be noticed, can so elaborate a "should" meme that it is analogous to some known biochemical excesses. For example, there is a weed killer used in lawns and gardens that works by causing such an intense growth rate in particular weed that the cells burst and the plants die. The replication of cells operates so intensely that the cells multiply and expand so fast that they burst and the whole plant dies.

Social memes that are not corrected by ongoing-shared human experience lead to similar excesses. Secrecy, or withholding information, causes excesses of just that kind—the Salem witch trials, the rise of Hitler, the McCarthy era of US history, the War on Drugs, the War on Terrorism, all wars on all demonized meme transgressors, etc.—all come from memes that ran away with themselves until they finally burst or got busted.

Without systems of correction, most of the humans used by whatever more efficient secretive meme complex replicator that happens to be the style of the time, usually try to kill unbelievers and often are themselves eventually killed by the belief they serve. The eventual hysterical growth of the meme often does finally kill it, and a lot of human beings who either carried or opposed it are usually killed at the same time. In the end, most of these meme-plexes have died from their own excesses because when they final-

Chapter THIRTY   The Memonic Plague

ly came to light, they either violated the truth of experience or eventually violated too many other memes in the human meme complexes of the time.

But when the humans who are left standing finally rid themselves of a previous meme complex system that had become so destructive to their friends, they replace it quickly with another, they then attach to that one to defend and propagate, and the process continues. Female circumcision comes to mind: a meme complex developed that valued cutting the clitoris out of young girls by their mothers because the women thought the men liked the idea and they ought to please the men. It was alive and thriving among a large group of humans in North Africa for a long time, and still exists today, but appears to be dying out slowly as it gets replaced by other fundamentalisms, possibly less painful and destructive to the lives of young girls.

This meme that is currently using my brain to advocate itself, a meme called something like "contextual perspective" or "a meme of memes" as Susan Blackmore calls it, can be used to (1) reflect on past memes that are now transcended (like blood letting or nationalism). It can also be used to (2) question current beliefs. And it can also be used (3) in anticipation of upcoming possibilities. Because of our ability to be aware of these ideas from a transcendent perspective looking backwards at history, there is the possibility of looking forward to the future with the same perspective. Radical honesty is clearly a meme whose time has come, because it is about this process of ongoing meme complex revolutions as a meme complex itself. It is suggested as a permanent alternative to the withholding meme complex. (Maybe if we get good at this we can do technological upgrades to former memeplexes like replacing computer parts. Revisions can come in little plug in packets, or changes of memory boards, or by modifications or reversals of function of sub parts of motherboards. Somebody stop me!!)

This "ongoing meme revision memeplex" could become one of those simple and obvious memeplexes that, once known, seems to have been there all along because it is hard to see how any dummy could have missed it. When the descriptive truth of awareness of what occurs in the world is shared, and along with it the honest sharing of interpretation of the meaning a person is making out of events, correction of out of control secret meme growth happens more frequently. This time-saver could be worth whole lifetimes spent in cul-de-sacs of memeland.

This, as it turns out, is also the fundamental principle of democracy. Throw it all out there in the public domain and let's not mummify our memes. The meme of "noticing" that transcends lesser memes allows for some participation by individual human consciousnesses in the ongoing meme complex evolution. The more minds the merrier. The more people to notice what is so in the world and apply their existing meme scheme assessments, the more of an opportunity for shared public correction of direction. This is, I think, what my friend Tom Atlee means by co-intelligence (see *The Tao of Democracy*).

How can this be applied when living into the future and dealing with, particularly, current conflicts between meme complexes? Take for example, Israel and Palestine or the American so-called "war on terrorism." What is fundamentally clear from what we have said so far, is that secrecy, withholding and lying are contrary to the greater power of transcendence through awareness and sharing. Yet secrecy is the very heart of the competition between nations relying on so-called "military intelligence" (a contradiction in terms). Secret interpretations of intentions of the other side are made by each side based on spying and other so-called "intelligence," resulting in conflicts between groups based on imaginings. "Secret intelligence" and true believership in ideals is the key to ongoing unresolved conflict—essentially a permanent state of war.

The first step to transcendence of the ongoing social disease of secret-keepers in authority is to doubt the validity of anything from authorities—any authorities whatsoever. However, the meme complex that is involved in always reacting to authority with certainty that authority must be wrong is equally a trap. What is hard to do, is to question authority with the freedom to obey or disobey. That is harder to do when we have been trained with years of schooling to obey a gigantic meme complex we could call "respect for authority and honoring of the ideas of the past" This huge meme complex has been passed on to us by finger pointing, ruler wielding, flag waving, moralizing, brainwashing teachers, parents, peers, and pundits, who are themselves thoroughly infected by the "kiss the ass of authority and preserve the illusion of freedom" meme complex. We have also had teachers of rebellion against that complex. The confusion and internal conflict that comes from our attempt to preserve our self–meme is pathetic, sad, stupid and hilarious at the same time. I think this is why Tibetan woodcuts of enlightened teachers often show them with expressions on their faces as if they are laughing and crying at the same time.

How do we observe meme complexes themselves with enough detachment not to be controlled by obedience or resistance to them? One of the answers to that question is that what we can laugh at and deride, we can also value and revise. One of the ways you know your memes have been confronted is when you get offended. Then after a while, you laugh. I hope this happens to you when you read the next chapter.

31

Comedians: Heroes of Meme Correction Through Hilarious Bitterness

Take George Carlin. (Please!) Here is a master of meme contrast who dares to confront conventional memes. George Carlin is a wise man who predicted present dilemmas quite some time back. Here is a meme-orable recent rap by Carlin, which stands in contrast to the history lessons taught in schools and edited on an ongoing basis by the media and other current meme complex maintenance people. Because of his humor, he allows us to look again at conventional interpretations (traditional memes) with empathy and cynicism at the same time, leaving an opening for ongoing revision of those meme complexes that run our lives.

Here's George Carlin on Bush War (the first one).

Rockets and Penises in the Persian Gulf

"History Lesson: I'd like to talk a little about that 'war' we had in the Persian Gulf. Remember that? The big war in the Persian

Gulf? Lemme tell you what was goin' on. Naturally, you can forget all that entertaining fiction about having to defend the model democracy those lucky Kuwaitis get to live under. And for the moment you can also put aside the very real, periodic need Americans have for testing their new weapons on human flesh. And also, just for the fun of it, let's ignore George Bush Sr.'s obligation to protect the oil interests of his family and friends. There was another, much more important, consideration at work. Here's what really happened.

Dropping a Load for Uncle Sam

"The simple fact is that America was long overdue to drop high explosives on helpless civilians; people who have no argument with us whatsoever. After all, it had been awhile, and the hunger gnaws. Remember that's our specialty: picking on countries that have marginally effective air forces. Yugoslavia is another, more recent example. But all that aside, let me tell you what I liked about that Gulf War: it was the first war that appeared on every television channel, including cable. And even though the TV show consisted largely of Pentagon war criminals displaying maps and charts, it got very good ratings. And that makes sense, because we like war. We're a warlike people. We can't stand not to be fucking with someone. We couldn't wait for the Cold War to end so we could climb into the big Arab sandbox and play with our nice new toys. We enjoy war. And one reason we enjoy it is that we're good at it. You know why we're good at it? Because we get a lot of practice. This country is only 200 years old, and already we've had ten major wars. We average a major war every twenty years, so we're good at it! And it's just as well we are, because we're not very good at anything else. Can't build a decent car anymore. Can't make a TV set, a cell phone, or a VCR. Got no steel industry left. No textiles. Can't educate our young people. Can't get health care to our old people. But we can bomb the shit outta your country, all right. We can bomb the shit outta your country!

If You're Brown, You're Goin' Down

"Especially if your country is full of brown people. Oh, we like that, don't we? That's our hobby now. But it's also our new job in the world: bombing brown people. Iraq, Panama, Grenada, Libya. You got some brown people in your country? Tell 'em to watch the fuck out, or we'll goddamn bomb them! Well, who were the last white people you can remember that we bombed? In fact, can you remember any white people we ever bombed? The Germans! That's it! Those are the only ones. And that was only because they were tryin' to cut in on our action. They wanted to dominate the world. Bullshit! That's our job. That's our fuckin' job. But the Germans are ancient history. These days, we only bomb brown people. And not because they're cutting in our action; we do it because they're brown. Even those Serbs we bombed in Yugoslavia aren't really white, are they? Naaah! They're sort of down near the swarthy end of the white spectrum. Just brown enough to bomb. I'm still waiting for the day we bomb the English. People who really deserve it.

A Disobedient American

Now you folks might've noticed, I don't feel about that Gulf War the way we were instructed to feel about it by the United States government. My mind doesn't work that way. You see, I've got this real moron thing I do, it's called 'Thinking.' And I guess I'm not a very good American, because I like to form my own opinions; I don't just roll over when I'm told. Most Americans roll over on command. Not me; I observe some preliminary rules.

"Believe you me, my first rule: I never believe what any authority says. None of them. Government, police, clergy, the corporate criminals. None of them. And neither do I believe anything I'm told by the media who, in the case of the Gulf War, functioned as little more than unpaid employees of the Defense Department, and who, most of the time, operate as an unofficial public relations agency for the government and industry. I don't believe any of them. And I have to tell you, folks, I don't really believe very much in my country either. I don't get all choked up about yellow ribbons and American flags. I see them as symbols, and I leave them to the symbol-minded. Show us your Dick.

"I also look at war itself a little differently from most. I see it largely as an exercise in dick-waving. That's really all it is: a lot of men standing around in a field waving their dicks at one another. Men, insecure about the size of their penises, choose to kill one another. That's also what all that moron athlete bullshit is all about, and what that macho, male posturing and strutting around in bars and locker rooms represents. It's called 'dick fear.' Men are terrified that their dicks are inadequate, and so they have to 'compete' in order to feel better about themselves. And since war is the ultimate competition, essentially men are killing one another in order to improve their genital self-esteem. You needn't be a historian or a political scientist to see the Bigger Dick Foreign Policy Theory at work. It goes like this: 'What? They have bigger dicks? Bomb them!' And of course, the bombs, the rockets, and the bullets are all shaped like penises. Phallic weapons. There's an unconscious need to project the national penis into the affairs of others. It's called 'fucking with people'

Show us your Bush

"So as far as I'm concerned, that whole thing in the Persian Gulf was nothing more than one big dick-waving cockfight. In this particular case, Saddam Hussein questioned the size of George Bush's dick. And George Bush had been called a wimp for so long, he apparently felt the need to act out his manhood fantasies by sending America's white children to kill other people's brown children. Clearly the worst kind of wimp. Even his name, 'Bush', as slang, is related to the genitals without being the genitals. A bush is a sort of passive, secondary sex characteristic. It's even used as a slang term for women: 'Hey, pal, how's the bush in this area?' I can't help thinking, if this president's name had been George Boner...well, he might have felt a little better about himself, and he wouldn't have had to kill all those children. Too bad he couldn't locate his manhood.

Premature Extraction

"Actually, when you think about it, this country has had a manhood problem for some time. You can tell the language we use; language always gives us away. What did we do wrong in Vietnam? We 'pulled out'! Not a very manly thing to do. No. When you're fucking people, you're supposed to stay with it and fuck them good; fuck them to death; hang in there and keep fucking them until they're all fucking dead. But in Vietnam what happened was by accident we left a few women and children alive, and we haven't felt good about ourselves since. That's why, in the Persian Gulf, George Bush had to say, 'This will not be another Vietnam.' He actually said, 'this time we're going all the way.' Imagine. An American president using the sexual slang of a thirteen-year-old to describe his foreign policy. And, of course, when it got right down to it, he didn't 'go all the way.' Faced with going into Baghdad he punked out. No balls. Just Bush. Instead, he applied sanctions, so he'd be sure that an extra half a million brown children would die. And so his oil buddies could continue to fill their pockets. If you want to know what happened in the Persian Gulf, just remember the first names of the two men who ran that war: Dick Cheney and Colin Powell. Dick and Colon. Someone got fucked in the ass. And those brown people better make sure they keep their pants on, because Dick and Colin have come back for an encore."

There you have it. Comedians like George Carlin not only challenge conventional memes, they violate them to stand as an example that one can do so and even create new memes of their own. So now we must bring this book to an end, summarize and do some memeplex recreation of our own. You can find more information and more wisdom from George Carlin at http://www.georgecarlin.com.

32

The Problem
With Secrecy

"I know a fella, got a lot to lose
Pretty nice fella, kinda confused
Got muscles in his head, never been used
Thinks he owns half of this town.
He drinks too much, and gets a big red nose
Then he beats his old lady with a rubber hose
Then he takes her out to dinner and buys her some clothes...
That's the way the world goes 'round."

"That's the way the world goes 'round
You're up one day, the next you're down.
Half an inch of water, and you think you're gonna drown.
That's the way the world goes 'round."

—John Prine

People are occupied and run by meme complexes that do not get altered or challenged, and therefore have little chance of being replaced, because of secrecy. This is the way incredible ignorance maintains itself. This is the secret to true believership and patriotism. One meme central to the ongoing life of the memeplex is the meme that preserves the illusion, in the mind of any person, that they are free. People who think they are not owned and operated by the meme complexes that actually own and operate them, maintain this mutual illusion by not telling each other the truth. Maintenance of traditional memeplexes depends upon secrecy.

We could call this currently maintained and nationally agreed upon meme complex here in the Western Hemisphere, the "incorrect freedom meme," or something like that. Currently there are many groups of people lost in memeland without a clue, who "think" they are in the land of the free and brave etc. Currently these are the people who have access to immense power to destroy groups and habitats of other groups; these other groups have the same limitation of perspective, but slightly different secondary meme complexes, and less power. What usually results is a lot of poorer folks with alternative limited meme complexes get killed and oppressed by the folks with the money.

The greatest problem of all with secrecy is that the conflict that happens according to the dictates of the memes in charge, persists and repeats itself in a predictable fashion because, since actions are based on information and ideas that are kept are secret except for a limited (and I do mean limited) few, they don't get revised. The cover story changes, but the underlying (under lying!!) structure remains the same. For example, secrecy, about the plutocratic operations done to maintain the illusion of democracy memeplex, is a requirement for its maintenance. So the same corporate entities fund the campaigns of both Democrats and Republicans so that whoever wins, the same folks are still in charge and keep making more money through weapons sales to our own government and the world. (Weapons manufacturers in the United States and Britain make 70% of all the weapons made and sold in the world).

The most pernicious form of lying is withholding what one knows to be true. What one knows to be true is based on observation—not on interpretation. (Although one may observe one's interpretation and report it.) Usually, observing and reporting doesn't happen. Instead, people report interpretations as though they were observed reality. And that's the way the world goes 'round. People withhold from reporting honestly what they do and think and feel, and they tell a story with various alternative interpretations to justify maintaining things as they are, or as they think they were, or should be. On an individual level this is called defensiveness. On a social level it is called the Department of Defense. That memeplex is an endless source of suffering. I have two suggestions for unzipping that memeplex.

The Truth Machine

One thing that would help with this problem would be the dependable capability to determine when people are actually lying, withholding or keeping secrets, on purpose. If we could reliably reveal to the world that people are lying when they are lying, or that they are telling the truth when they are telling the truth, anyone could challenge anyone to take the test. We need a Truth Machine. We need some people who are aware of the meme meme to design and be a part of a series of tests that reveal secret and hidden memes with great reliability.

By using technical equipment and expertise developed in part by several of our 36 secret intelligence organizations, and employing empaths (sensitive and perceptive humans—psychotherapists and teachers and perceptive people) in sequence, we could tell when people are lying or withholding. To constantly undo lying and secrecy we could build a system to free folks from limiting meme complexes which heretofore have never been really touched by general conscious awareness. This would not just be a threat to liars, withholders and secret keepers, it would also open up tremendous freedom, which would, in turn, threaten everyone's illusion of who they are. So it's a hard sell. But wouldn't it be great if we could share what is going on with each other in ways we never have had any memes of doing before?

When we know that we can determine when people are lying there occurs at the same time a permission for people be honest — about themselves and in their dealings with each other. (Since they know that the truth can, and probably will, be found out, they might as well tell the truth in the first place.) This could be a boon to humankind.

There is a science fiction novel by James Halperin called *The Truth Machine*. In this story, Halperin envisions a future transformed world, which comes about as the result of building a device that is 100% reliable in telling when people are lying. The tremendous possible benefit to the people of the world (to protect them from themselves) is expressed by one of the characters in the novel, who says, in casual conversation: "Back when I was in Middlesex, my friend Tilly told me a story about her six-year-old cousin who burned himself to death playing with matches. In a way, that's what we humans are — children playing with matches. We have overpowering technology and weapons of destruction, yet we lack the discretion to use them wisely. We have to find a way to change our character, to keep us from starting fires that could incinerate us all. I think a Truth Machine offers the best hope." (*The Truth Machine,* James Halperin, pp. 182-183.)

I am putting into motion the building of a Truth Machine, using a combination of perceptive people and technological devices and people skilled in using the devices. Anyone interested in helping can contact me for further information about this (brad@radicalhonesty.com).

The Campaign Against Secrecy

Neale Donald Walsch (author of the *Conversations with God* books) and I have become good friends out of our common commitment to a spiritual revolution brought about through personal honesty. We have both found in our work, that once people have the courage to take responsibility for honesty in relationships, they do, in fact, have happier lives. So we made public a videotaped conversation about our agreement on the topic, and then published a book, *Honest to God: A Change of Heart That Can Change the World.* Out of that conversation we have started the Campaign Against Secrecy. We are collecting together our colleagues who we know are committed to helping people, and engaging in political action with them (see www.changeofheart.biz).

We believe that it is possible not only to improve the quality of individual lives, moment to moment, but also make changes worldwide that will transform the structures that keep suffering in place. We believe that lying is the primary source of human suffering. And we believe in the healing power of honesty.

We propose to all human beings that we reorganize the world based on compassion for each other that comes from honesty, and the love of being, rather than our current system of organization based on defense of property.

We are making up a list of people who have the heart to change the way we do things. We are making a list of people who have heart, who we think we could talk into running for President of the United States, and who would have a chance to win. Please feel free to add to the list. (www.changeofheart.biz). We hope that if we offer enough support, these possible candidates for President of the United States will have the courage to tell the truth and to oppose all advocates of secrecy. We are convinced that the primary secret of how to maintain enough imbalances in the world to continue to maintain control of the economic order by those who currently control it, is secrecy itself. The primary secret is secrecy. The primary secret to maintaining control is secrecy. We are looking for people to hold public office who will risk trusting us all with the truth.

There are 37 separate secret agencies funded by the United States government. The CIA, perhaps the largest and most well-funded secret terrorist organization in the world, is only one of them. There are 36 more and a new one was just added in 2002 called "Homeland Security." We pay for them, but we don't get to see their budgets. Their budgets are supervised by three or four congress people, who were elected by popular vote, bought with commercials paid for by folks with a vested financial interest in maintaining defensiveness.

We say that there are enough people in the United States who are on a spiritual path, or invested in personal growth, or socially active in movements for ecological, educational and economic justice, all of whom are fed up with being lied to and having information withheld from them, that we could actually win an election for president, and re-establish a two-party system again in the United States. To do this we must override the influence of corporate money by the numbers of folks enrolled in the idea of actual democracy. Then we must establish full public financing of all elections making it illegal for any group of people to give more than a hundred dollars in support of any candidate; this would give democracy at least a fighting chance, on an ongoing basis, to bring about an end to the plutocracy that has kept us locked into a wartime economy for over a hundred years.

Toward that end I am going to do several things personally: (1) I am running for Congress from the 7th District of Virginia in 2004; (2) I will campaign at the same time I campaign for myself, for a candidate for President who supports actual democracy: Dennis Kucinich; and (3) I will publish this book and several others in The Truthtellers series, (one of the next of which will be *The Truthtellers: Stories of Success by Honest People in Politics*). Please contact me through one of the following three web sites if you want to help with any or all of these efforts: www.radicalhonesty.com, www.usob.org, or www.changeofheart.biz.

Political Action to Counter Current Conventional Meme Complexes and to Set Up Conscious Meme Modification Systems

This excerpt is from Robert Thurman's book *Inner Revolution*, about a political agenda based on enlightenment: "The worldwide great shift of wealth and power to the top stratum of individuals has been immensely destructive to the delicate weave of most industrial societies. The fake politicians always show themselves in front of slamming jail doors, throwing switches on electric chairs, building lots of cells, and arming cops with automatic weapons — all measures taken against the already poor and oppressed. Our platform must show a real commitment to justice for all....

"A bodhisattva or messianic person wants to accumulate wealth so he or she can give it away to needy people, most creatively by investing intelligently in things that will provide long-term happiness to the people. But if wealth becomes an object of obsession, if it is used carelessly, it can be incredibly destructive, most of all to the wealthy people themselves. The enlightened democratic system institutionalizes revolution and uses progressive income taxes and other mechanisms to rebalance the rich/poor equation gently and continuously. Our platform reaffirms this policy of continuous, peaceful revolution out of compassion for both the poor and the rich. True wealth is a rich network of loving people, a pleasant and healthy lifestyle, a beautiful environment, and an inviting setting for expressing creativity. Money alone is a heavy burden, isolating its owner from real affection, ennobling unhealthy addictions, harming the environment, and causing boredom, frustration, and anxiety. Enlightenment cures all these problems through its prime virtue: generosity in all things."

The Compassionate Revolution

The revolution referred to in that quote from Thurman, and in the brilliant book by Dave Edwards called *The Compassionate Revolution,* could be called an "ongoing meme revision" revolution. It should be clear by now that my friends and I are asserting that the usual either/or, or us vs. them memeplex can be transcended through generous sharing of the truth. In former days we were forced to choose between either compassion or greed in both our personal and social life. That is and always has been an impossible choice. But if we acknowledge that every compassionate person is greedy and every greedy person compassionate, and we all have both, could we not, instead of making it either/or, simply make compassion the higher value and greed the secondary one? Then could we not build that into our economic and political structures?

When we have even had a choice in an either/or world between people whose first priority is greed and people whose first priority is compassion, more often that not the greedy one has won because he or she had more money to pay for their campaign. Greed has been ahead for many years now, but the greater awareness we are growing into together, focused on a campaign against secrecy, could make greed eventually into a structurally established consideration secondary to compassion.

If greed and compassion are permanently a part of us, a balance between the two must now be accomplished by the being called mankind. The courage for telling the truth about what is so must win out, until the conclusion is assented to by all people, that we are of one cloth and honor each others' humanity above the pleasures and sufferings of conquest and control.

The Truthtellers

The current, antiquated political and economic structures are based on secrecy and greed more than compassion. We have been operating from a memeplex that is now too constraining, that is based on a more limited definition of who we are. The flag we salute must now have a picture of the world on it. Patriotism for a collection of less than all of us is a paradigm we can no longer afford. Homeland security can only be accomplished if we consider the whole world our homeland.

Radical Honesty is the meme whose time has come. Ending secrecy and sharing honestly on both the personal and social level can bring about an end to the massive economic imbalance that keeps the poor getting poorer and the rich getting richer. The secrecy and lying that is structurally permitted by the legal, economic and political system worldwide is the primary source of ecological disaster, the perpetuation of the military industrial complex, war, poverty and terrorism. The end of these abominations is the beginning of heaven on earth. We are committed to bringing that about. It comes about, we think, through incremental increases in openness and honesty. That is our faith and our common cause.

33

This Is What We Meme by "We Are All One"

"Instead of a 'Brain Trust' we need a 'Soul Trust' to execute the affairs of the new 'shadow busters.' All it takes is enough light, and the shadow disappears."
— Alan Hutner of Transitions Media

Thank you so much for reading this book. I know you had to go through a big shift from short, personal stories of change and transformation to very complex, but exciting hard work on the transcendent perspective of memes. Thank you. This is the last chapter. I write these final words directly to you who have followed the whole trail and trial of this work to this point.

The replicator Alligator and the meme dream virus are afoot in the brains of humans. A bunch of us have got the bug and are on the prowl. We are being used by the oneness memes and we have volunteered to be used by them. We invite you to try it with us on purpose. Resistance is futile. These "democracy," "shared truth of experience" and "interpretation for the sake of liberation from interpretation" memes are very good memeplexes. Come on in.

The ocean of memes is fine. Swim on in and maybe we won't drown if we keep an eye out for each other's safety.

Based on what people have shared in this book I think we can operate from some rules of thumb about how we protect our noticing being, and each other, as we re-meme-ber who we are:

- Say what you really meme. (Be honest).

Acknowledge that every meme is a memes to an end. Say what end your meme is a meme to. (Be open. Don't have any hidden agendas).

- Deepen the meme-ing of consciousness. We have to listen to each other to do this. We have to be open to discovering, through sharing with each other, memes that we were not aware of. (Be engaged, make corrections of your mind from your heart out of being continually related honestly to other people you have let yourself love).

- Grounding in the experience of noticing and identifying ourselves as noticers and meme makers as our fundamental identity, can become familiar and we can settle into it. Then, new ideas are less threatening to the memeplex we call our "self." We can agree to explicit memes established together as our shared vision for the future. Then the ongoing conversation about our shared vision can be used to revise less explicit memes that are familiar to us, and fundamental to our beliefs about who we are, yet are comparatively dysfunctional. We can help each other through that. That also keeps the ongoing meme change revolution we carry forth an adventure rather than a threat. (Be conscious and willing to admit attachment to personal memes, compare them to memes agreed upon and chosen and held conscious through ongoing conversation with friends, and get over your attachment to your dysfunctional "self"-protective beliefs).

- Make a lot of jokes about the memes we think run us, and the memes that really do. Laugh or cry or get pissed off and share it each time we lose or misplace or ruin a meme we thought was critical to who we were. (They don't call wisecracks wisecracks for nothing! They are cracks in memeplex jails! Be in a somewhat harsh but funny therapeutic community with other human being memeing-makers).

• Re-meme-ber the Alamo. Consider heroes as idiots and vice versa. Constantly question and review history, both personal and collective, with the meme meme as your perspective. Use meme meme scheme as an alternative to automatic belief and as a tool to liberate your mind and our minds and our collective mind from previously more limited memes. (Constantly revise history through constantly revising your perspective on history and our perspective on history).

• Let parenting and teaching become meme replicator tasks, to be done on purpose, consciously, to manifest the best love we can to our children. This is a scary task to do consciously for those of us just awakening. We must share our fear, experience it, feel our way through it and move on. (This means group therapy for parents available at all times, family therapy for the kids and their parents on an ongoing basis whenever they want—life in a therapeutic community).

• We must re-meme our context for mind altering substances like psychedelic drugs and drugs that produce varying degrees of altered states of consciousness. To consider their value in terms of the meme meme could change "the war on drugs" which is done completely out of fear, to the use of drugs in ongoing education, and for the enhancement of our lives together through what we learn in altered states of consciousness. It is scary, but we could accept drug-induced alterations in consciousness as opportunities for re-tuning memes, and expanding what we meme by memes, and for improving our lives together. (Families and friends could do mind altering-drugs together now and then, on purpose, in order to learn together, and then share it with the world).

• Expand what we meme by all memes. (We are all gods together. We create the world together by simply perceiving it together, and we can participate in the memosphere together on purpose—if you know what I meme.)

We know that people who get over being hurt and angry are people who get to forgiveness, and they do that by telling the truth. These are also people who can become powerful in changing the way the world works.

Nothing could be scarier than this. We really need each other in order to do this. We really need each other to be able to do this. From every relationship we have, from personal to global, lying and secretiveness keep us in a small jail. Only truthfulness will set us free. Or if not, at least we can take over the bigger prison.

Thank you for hearing all these stories. Please pass them forward.

Love,

Brad Blanton

brad@radicalhonesty.com

Bibliography

The Compassionate Revolution by David Edwards—A book on the beginning of the world's integration of Buddhism (as are Dave Edwards' other books).

The Tao of Democracy by Tom Atlee—An articulation of co-intelligence.

Radical Honesty by Brad Blanton—The source book for personal psychological freedom through honesty.

Practicing Radical Honesty by Brad Blanton—The meditation in action book for practicing Radical Honesty.

Honest to God by Neale Donald Walsch and Brad Blanton—The initial integration of personal growth, spiritual growth and social action.

Radical Parenting by Brad Blanton—A synthesis of the great goal of compassion from Buddhism, modern neurological science, and hands-on application of spiritual principles to child rearing and self re-parenting.

A Language Older Than Words by Derrick Jensen—The definitive work on the dissociative path of civilization and our common insanity.

Neither Wolf Nor Dog—The very best of our Native American wisdom heritage.

The Culture of Make Believe—by Derrick Jensen.

If there seems to be a gap between what the enlightenment books describe and what you find in your own life, if you still think enlightenment is something that will happen to you in the future (or not at all), if you're still chasing experiences and self-improvement, then this book may be just what you need to wake up to the truth that what you are seeking is already here. *Awake in the Heartland* by Joan Tollifson is an honest book about waking up now, right here in the midst of ordinary life.

Send Us Your Story

We assert that the power to create your own story is inversely related to how trapped you are in a previous story. Further, a lot of lying is considered natural in the average life of the well-acculturated—and this goes for almost any culture. The kind of story that most of us live in, came from our survival techniques developed in childhood and adolescence, involves lying and withholding within the context of the cultural story in which we were raised.

People who have risen above their programming through practicing what we preach, all have stories to tell about how they escaped the stories that used to imprison them. The stories are about how getting honest in their lives has turned their lives around. They are good stories. We believe that good stories about honesty cause more good stories about honesty to show up. So we have a plan, not only to run workshops where these stories get told in person, but also to put more and more of these stories out there for other people to hear and learn about. We want to spread these stories around to encourage and inspire growing numbers of people to try practicing radical honesty. This way we will start a veritable plague of stories and cause still further inspiration. Once we demonstrate that this is not only a practical but freeing way to live, with enough stories in which people prove the point, Radical Honesty will become an idea whose time has come and the world will change because of this work. That's our plan and we're sticking to it.

This book is the first in a series. If you have a story to share, please send it to us so we can put it in the next volume. All you have to do is tell the truth, change your life, and tell us that story. Click on www.radicalhonesty.com then e-mail us about sending in your story; or call us at 1 800 EL TRUTH. Thanks.